THE
SHELL GAME

*Reflections on Rowing and
the Pursuit of Excellence*

STEPHEN KIESLING

WILLIAM MORROW AND COMPANY, INC.

New York   1982

Library of Congress Cataloging in Publication Data

Kiesling, Stephen.
   The shell game.

   1. Kiesling, Stephen. 2. Rowers—United States
—Biography. 3. Yale University—Rowing. I. Title.
GV790.92.K53A37   797.1'23'0924 [B]   81-14187
                                        AACR2
ISBN 0-688-00958-1

Printed in the United States of America

First Edition

1 2 3 4 5 6 7 8 9 10

For

STROKE	*John*
7	*Matthew*
6	*Andy*
5	*Eric*
4	*Dave*
3	*Karl*
2	*Joe*
BOW	*Ted*
COXSWAIN	*Andy*
AND	*Tony*

Contents

THE
SHELL GAME

Preface

I remember meeting the Russians in September of 1979 at the World Rowing Championships in Bled, Yugoslavia. They had nice sweat suits. Blue, with CCCP in white block letters across the back—not so nice as the French Adidas sweat suits, but Frenchmen were difficult traders. The Russians would exchange a sweat suit for a couple pairs of Levi's jeans or, if you were really cagey, a ten-dollar calculator and a Kennedy half-dollar.

Not only did the Russians have nice equipment but they rowed fast: perhaps not so fast as the East Germans, but they beat us. No doubt they were all professionals in disguise: cloned, steroid-injected automatons—who happened to row beautifully and win most of the medals.

Athletics seemed more serious to the East Germans than they did to the Russians. I don't think the Easties were supposed to talk to us. I know that they were forbidden to trade equipment. After the finals the competitors gathered at the boat tents to trade shirts, sweats and whatnot. The East Germans did not participate. However, they lived across the hall from us in the hotel. The night after the finals a gargantuan Eastie came to the door, roaring drunk. I am 6 feet 4 inches and looked him straight in the chin. Did we have dollars? he inquired in a slur of butchered English. Dollars we had, but he kept pointing to his crotch and winking. He winked again before doubling over in laughter. Only then did I spot the orange-and-black sash of his racing shirt protruding above his belt.

Would we buy a racing shirt for fifteen dollars? he managed to ask. A sweat suit for twenty-five? I tried to look dubious, but failed. Gleefully, he shushed us and swayed on tiptoe toward the curtains. "Spies are everywhere," he was just able to convey as 230 drunken pounds of tiptoeing oarsman fell sprawling over the coffee table.

("What happened?" the hotel maid would ask, pointing to the remains of the table.

"Spies!" we would chant in unison.)

Meanwhile, our defector closed the curtains and dimmed the lights before extracting his wares. Immediately the bargaining began.

Rookies to the U.S. team like me had been carefully briefed on trading well before we reached Yugoslavia. I had been warned, for example, that although the Russians did not have the highest-quality gear, anticipation of the Olympics would make it expensive. New Zealand and West German gear was both handsome and scarce so that too would be expensive. There were also problems to watch for when trading with some countries. Polish and Czechoslovakian gear was not colorfast. Japanese and Egyptian gear was generally too small, and

Italian shirts tended to shrink. With the French one had to be especially careful. French oarswomen were known to take men aside, point to whatever they wanted, and then peel off their own shirts. It took great presence of mind to bargain with a half-naked Frenchwoman.

The East Germans alone sold equipment—supposedly because they were not permitted to wear clothes from another country; however, after we offered a pair of Levi's, it became obvious that our Eastie was interested only in our dollars. "Fifteen dollars," he repeated eagerly, pointing to the wad of bills that I pulled from the bottom of my duffel bag.

Behind the Iron Curtain, dollars are worth many times the legal exchange rate on the black market because they provide access to Western luxuries; but even at the legal exchange rate his prices were grossly inflated. If a Russian sweat suit could be traded for a ten-dollar calculator, then fifteen dollars should have bought more than a shirt—even a world champion's shirt; in the drunken darkness, however, one couldn't tell dollars from local dinars. He kept smiling and nodding as I piled a five-dollar bill, a couple of singles, ten Yugoslavian dinars, and a laundry ticket into his outstretched palm. Unfortunately, neither did I see that his shirt could have sheltered a medium-sized rhino. He liked Americans, he said, crushing my hand affectionately after the deal; he didn't like Russians, but he liked Americans. Would I care to buy a set of sculling blades? A hundred dollars behind the boat tents and they were mine. How about a "single" (a one-man shell) for eight hundred? He gave me his club pin, which I stuck on my sweat shirt next to the Russian pin depicting Misha, the Olympic bear, rowing a shell—my good-luck charm to help me stay on the team for Moscow.

That was the politics of athletics at the World Championships in Yugoslavia—except, of course, for the squadrons of black-clad militia who whirred about on motorcycles. Wraiths, like the couriers from Hades in the movie *Orpheus,* they remained polite even after I was arrested.

I wouldn't have dared to climb that pole, but as we strolled back to the hotel at about nine o'clock one night, someone scurried from the hedgerow, leaped for a light pole, climbed the requisite fifteen feet, and pilfered two of the striking blue-and-white regatta flags. Realizing that civic duty demanded we stop the perpetrator and that catching him was safer than climbing a pole ourselves, we gave chase. As it turned out, we chased a couple of American scullers. Disgusted, I trotted back to the next pole and shinned up. Not until I had wrenched the wooden flagstaffs out of their sockets in the light pole did I notice the headlights from what had appeared to be an unoccupied Renault. How could I have known that the pole was a militia stakeout? My two comrades, who had stationed themselves along the roadway to watch for such an eventuality, recognized the trap and did not hesitate. There were only two spare oarsmen on the squad, so if all three of us were put in jail, at least one boat would have been unable to race— an international incident that could have disgraced our entire country. "Personal relationships cannot come before the needs of the nation," they reasoned with newfound national stoicism, disappearing into the hedgerow. Fortunately, the militia were willing to negotiate. They took my flags and sent me to bed with the promise of thirty days if they caught me again. That was politics.

*   *   *

I returned to New Haven for my senior year at Yale a week and a half into the fall term but had no class conflicts. I took no classes. Thirteen other seniors and I had been accepted as Scholars of the House. We were given credit for ten classes, our entire senior year, for a project. Among us were novelists, musicians, a computer wiz, a biologist, a Barbie Doll sociologist and I, an oarsman. My mission was to spend the year training for the 1980 Olympics and to write a thesis on the philosophy of sports.

In December of 1979, three months after I had returned from Yugoslavia and five months before the final selection of the Olympic team, Russia rolled into Afghanistan. That day I changed from ivory-tower potential Olympian to political pawn who feared he had conditioned himself as a first-round draft-choice—and not for the NFL.

With Carter's pronouncement of the boycott my artfully constructed retreat of rowing and writing burst apart. I was dazed, unable to believe or even comprehend that such an unlikely twist of events could destroy something that I had always assumed to be sacrosanct. As it turned out, however, I had only a brief time to worry about it.

In January of 1980, two of my classmates and I left New Haven to spend a week in Melbourne, Florida, training with the Olympic squad. As I got on the plane I was listless and fatalistic. Even though the final team would not be chosen until May, I had hardly bothered to practice during the days before we left, and I went half expecting to enjoy a week of vacation funded by the U.S. Olympic Committee. When I arrived and was whisked out to practice, it hardly bothered me that my boat was losing; in fact, I don't even believe I pulled hard. Not until the coach demanded that the two boats be brought together and that I switch from my seat in what had been the slower of the two boats to the opposite seat in what then became the slower boat did I realize that the boycott was only a political and not an athletic reality. If I had continued to believe in the boycott as an athletic reality, I would have been cut.

I had to earn my seat before worrying about a boycott; but in one important sense, this sounds like a much more painful dilemma than it actually was. Although the outside reality had changed, the goal for which we had worked had not changed in the slightest. To think that we trained several hours each day for three and a half years for just those few public minutes of racing is ridiculous. To reach for excellence, to work with the best, and to achieve those brief moments of perfection was priceless. The slightest possibility of proving to be the best before the entire world was irresistible, but being denied the chance could not derogate the preparation.

But I don't want to tell the tale of the boycott and I don't think anyone really wants to hear it. Sorting sour grapes is the business of historians, and as an athlete I am the antithesis of a historian. The Olympics and what happened to them was only the public tip of what is for athletes a very large and very private iceberg. This book is an attempt to chip away at one such iceberg, one that is distinct from others because it involves a strange and wonderful sport immersed so deeply in the equally strange and wonderful traditions of Yale University. This book is an excavation of athletics by one who was new to sports, one who grew up with an intellectual distance and even disdain for sports, came to Yale and subsequently was engulfed. Had I grown up as an athlete, as a jock, my story would involve only the sequence of competition that had enabled me to ascend the athletic ladder; but because I became a serious athlete relatively late, I think that I was more conscious of the process than my fellow Olympic athletes. I discovered as I made what seemed a dramatic turnabout from intense academics to intense athletics that the two were not so different. Dedicated dancers, scholars, oarsmen and executives are different in expression but not in intention.

This is not the *Ball Four* of training for the Olympics. It is a story about rowing at Yale. Originally I had hoped to give a perspective between academics and sports, but I realize that at the time I had no perspective. I could rewrite the story with hindsight, but it would be a completely different work.

The Catch

"Countdown from bow when ready!" The coxswain's voice cut the dawn mist, waking us back to the shell. Hurriedly, I finished tying my feet into the footstretchers and rolled my seat experimentally back and forth along the slide.

"Bow."

"Two."

"Three."

"Four!" I yelled as the count moved through me and up to number eight, the stroke oar. One by one we positioned ourselves at the top of the slide: legs cocked, arms outstretched, blades flat against the water.

"All eight to row, ready all...row!"

In one motion the eight oars flipped into the river, our backs opened and our legs straightened. Hesitantly, but then with more assurance, the boat surged into the current. We were all cold and stiff so early in the morning, yet with each stroke our bodies loosened, fell together. The boat, first pushing through the river, soon lifted with each catch to skim across the ripples as our movements lost self-consciousness to the easy flowing rhythm.

Past the finish line we paddled, past the Rock and past the Harvard camp at Red Top; the landmarks slipped by unnoticed to the beat of the oars. After each stroke, eight new whirlpools traced our path. I thought of nothing, wished for nothing but to put just a little more distance between one set of whirlpools and the next—to make the next stroke a little closer to perfection.

A patch of mist suffused the morning light. Then from nowhere came the rain: hard, driving, a counterpoint to the rhythmic splash of the oars. Their gray carbon fiber matched the water, matched the air. Eric's bare back moved in front of me, the triangle of his deltoids and lats coursing the rain. Surging water, flowing oars and a bare back moving rhythmically before me.

For those moments I could forget where I was, forget the coming race and immerse myself in the pure joy of motion. Then, as it had for every other practice here, the purpose of our efforts broke the harmony. We were no longer students in New Haven balancing rowing and studies. It was the beginning of summer in 1979. School was over and we were now full-time oarsmen. Three weeks earlier the crew had moved from the distractions of Yale to Gales Ferry for yet another chance to fulfill the goal that has obsessed Yale crews since 1852—to win the Race against Harvard. For more than one hundred years the Ferry has been home for Yale crews training for this one contest, the oldest and most tradition-laden intercollegiate athletic event in the United States. Not since 1962 had Yale won the race.

We had arrived at the Ferry during late afternoon. Most of the other thirty oarsmen had driven together straight from New Haven, but John Biglow, our stroke, and I had left a few hours before the others so that we could stop on our way and visit his grandmother in Old Lyme. John's late grandfather, Yale '07, had been the captain of the football team and had rowed in the four seat of the eight. Our visit was both social and a kind of pilgrimage to be blessed back into the tradition by someone who had lived it. At the time I had thought that it was wrong to make the jump to the Ferry, only an hour's bus ride but a hundred years of history, without this blessing.

John was of old Massachusetts stock, a third-generation Yalie whose ancestors had taught at both Yale and Harvard and who had relatives near all the major rowing courses in New England. He was a bit eccentric from impeccable breeding; his wide brown eyes and disarming frankness first gave the impression of complete innocence, but underneath he was orderly, and tense. He wouldn't be beaten. In the Yale Varsity Heavyweight eight of 1979 John was relatively small, only 6 feet 3 inches tall and 187 pounds, yet undoubtedly he was one of the finest oarsmen Yale had produced. He was lean and powerful with a stroke as meticulous as his habits. When we were freshmen two years back he had hated me. Having rowed for three years in prep school, he could not tolerate my inexperience, at least not in the same boat with him. Inexperience made me oblivious to my failings and that galled John most of all. In 1979 we were roommates, bitter rivals, and if friendship develops from shared experience, best friends—a friendship between duelists, the sort of friends who ensure that the other never performs below potential. It was something quite different from the "Do your own thing and I'll understand" friendships that I had grown up with, but I had come a long way from California.

Although not expecting us, John's grandmother seemed to sense our mission. Her welcome had been gracious yet expectant. A Spartan mother. Biglows, she informed me, were a special breed, and John was to be no exception. She led us across landscaped terraces through ancient rooms cluttered with memorabilia to the study that had been John's grandfather's. There on the wall amid an assortment of other athletic icons hung the banner from the 1907 football team. Grandma Biglow then told us a few brief tales about the successes of that football team, but when we asked about the eight she mentioned only that the boat of 1907 lost the Race. That fact I had known because the results of the Race are printed at the bottom of the photograph of each varsity eight that hangs in the dining room at Gales Ferry. Her point, however, struck home. If you don't win the Race, it really isn't something to talk about. In fact, if you lose the race, your team picture is not hung at the Ferry until the next crew wins. Somewhere there were a stack of fifteen photographs of the crews since 1962 waiting to be hung at Gales Ferry. With each loss the shame, the number of unremembered on the wall, and our stake in the race increased. John and I received our cookies, accepted her blessing, and continued our drive to the Ferry determined that our own eight would not be treated with the same silence in afteryears. Grandma Biglow went back to writing her class notes for the Smith College magazine. At ninety, she could not have had many classmates left to read them.

Gales Ferry commands a wooded promontory on the Thames River five miles from New London, Connecticut. From all appearances it is a small country club with a grand white clubhouse, a cottage for the manager, and a long boathouse mounted on pilings at the edge of the river—all kept locked eleven months out of the year, awaiting the end of school and the return of the next Yale Heavyweight crew.

After our visit with Grandma Biglow, however, our approach to the Ferry was nothing like arriving at a country club. With a mile to go we turned from the main road, trading the last shopping center for the eroded stone of the cemetery and the small white houses built by whaling captains. Minutes later we turned again at a plaque detailing the history of the Ferry and found ourselves bouncing down the familiar gravel road alongside the old Ferry building to the boathouse. The shell trailer had preceded us, and with its presence came the excitement of knowing that after eleven months the Ferry was once again alive. We leaped out and scurried to the trunk for our bags, but even as I opened the trunk I paused. John's glance was already transfixed down the river. Instinctively, I felt his thoughts, unconsciously mimicking his grimace before he squared his features and met my gaze. The smile did not come. Once again our gazes drifted down the river.

"I understand why Eric brings his Bible out here!" I said, half in jest, trying to break the mood, but as I said it I saw an unfamiliar flicker in John's eyes. Out there it was so easy to switch from triumph to fear.

Just on the horizon were the twin prongs of a highway bridge now wreathed in fog. The bridge began the distance that we would row—a distance that Harvard had rowed faster for the previous sixteen years. Four miles.

Twenty minutes. On paper it didn't seem that long—I understand that marathon runners keep going for hours—but then I remembered losing my shirt last year to the Harvard six man. We finished twelve seconds behind and pulled our boats together in fulfillment of the tradition. The tradition, however, did not mention what to do if your opponent was unconscious. He, the victor, was slumped forward on his slide, eyes blank, breathing shallowly between convulsions even as the launch arrived to hoist him from the shell. Each convulsion added to my guilt. He had given all and more than his body could withstand and for that dedication he had won. Four miles, twenty minutes and an unconscious six man.

The race last year had been agony. Our stroke, Dave Potter, had pulled a muscle in his back during the winter, and it flared up again in the harsh training before the Race. After practice he could not stand straight or even breathe deeply. Some nights I could hear Dave struggle for sleep, crying out when he moved too quickly or breathed too hard. The Yale health service told him not to row for two weeks and then try again. When Dave told them he had to row, that the boat could not practice effectively with a replacement, the doctors replied only that jury-rigging people was not their business. They did not understand the Race. Dave endured the pain and returned to practice.

On Race Day the pain had largely subsided, although we had no assurance that it would not return. We began the Race believing that we would need a superhuman effort to end the fifteen-year pall over Yale rowing, but we were scared. Hesitation put us a length behind in the first mile. Halfway through the Race, we made a desperate move to pull even, giving everything we had to take the lead. I suppose if we had taken back those last few seats we would have had more to give, but we moved no closer than two seat-lengths behind and slipped back.

Three miles into the Race, Dave was barely conscious. The stroke cadence, already low, was slipping. From 34 strokes per minute it fell to 32 and then to 31. Seeing his eyes glaze over, Andy, our coxswain, splashed him with water but managed to raise the cadence for only a few strokes. From the six seat I could feel the boat becoming sluggish, and I should have been able to maintain the rating, but somehow it would not happen. My legs moved up and pushed down stroke after stroke mechanically, the months given to training begging to be forgotten. No other Yalie had won this race in fifteen years. How did they expect us to win it? The two lengths separating us from Harvard could just as well have been miles. Perhaps that was why as a junior I was moved from the six seat to the four seat. Dave, although his back finally healed, was moved to the junior varsity.

My hands had clenched as I stared out toward the bridge. Nineteen seventy-nine would be different. We were no longer the upstarts who had surprised everyone by winning the Eastern Sprints for the first Yale championship in fifteen years. The eight of 1978 had been sophomores and juniors. In 1979 we were juniors and seniors. Stronger, fitter and more experienced, we averaged 6 feet 4 inches in height and 200 pounds in weight. Strutting along the docks before races, we no longer had to act to look confident and tough. Either the act had taken hold or we had forgotten that we were acting. I would have been frightened to race against us.

We had learned the perils of hubris. A year earlier that overweening pride had left us vulnerable, allowing the success of our best racing to convince us that we were unbeatable under any conditions. After most other athletic competitions, the loser shakes hands with the victor and is then free to slink back to the locker room. Rowing, however, is the classic gentlemen's sport and carries with it the classic gentlemen's wager. After the race, the loser shakes hands, peels off his sweat-soaked jersey, his skin, and hands it across. Naked to the waist, the loser congratulates the winner, who has carelessly slung his latest trophy over his left shoulder. After the Eastern Sprint Championships in 1978, I stood by the Yale boat trailer with a glass of champagne in my left hand while shaking hands and collecting shirts with my right. By the time we tied our boats back on the trailer for the return to New Haven, fourteen shirts were slung, dripping with others' sweat, over my left shoulder. Harvard, Princeton, Dartmouth, Navy: every rowing power in the East had been reduced to the amorphous, bare-backed crowd before us. To wear the shirts was to control the destiny of whomever we raced—or so we believed.

In addition to winning our opponents' shirts, we earned back the traditional Yale racing shirt with white trim and satin sash. In the early seventies, the cost of losing race after race had forced a change to cheap blue T-shirts with only a printed white *Y* on the breast. The return of those traditional shirts the week before the 1978 Eastern Championship, Yale's first victory in twenty years, made them seem a magical protection against losing. So convinced were we of our own invincibility that we had hardly bothered to prepare for our final 2,000-meter race against Dartmouth. Dartmouth, after all, had finished ninth in the Sprints, not even making the finals.

We met Dartmouth in the tumultuous waves of Lake Onondaga, New York. Gusting wind had made the lake almost unrowable, and someone remarked that Dartmouth should just give us their shirts to save us all a lot of trouble. We didn't get nervous until waves began pouring over the gunwales, and even then we did not insist on time to bail before the start. We flailed into our first defeat with a hundred pounds of displaced river crashing into the stern with every stroke.

We were now no longer new to success. We had been favored in all of our races and had fulfilled expectations by large margins. The year's preparation carried us at least three boat lengths ahead of any of our early competition. There was open water between our boat and Harvard's at the Sprints. After each race we would comment briefly on the strengths and weaknesses of the performance and then concentrate forward to the next test. After only a few days, the 1979 Eastern Championship was a faded memory. The captured shirts which I displayed so proudly the previous year were tossed into a bag and into the closet. We rowed for a single goal.

Wordlessly sharing our recollections, John and I turned, freeing our eyes to wander up the slope to the Ferry. Despite its peeling paint, Gales Ferry was still marvelously imposing. A friend of mine described the exterior of the varsity house as essentially a New England barn—a magnificent clapboard structure with Cape Cod latticed windows and a delicate gallery porch—but a barn nonetheless. I suppose she was right. The shape of the building was more than vaguely barn-like, but having experienced the place, I realize that from that same perspective the Arc de Triomphe must resemble a tollbooth. John and I moved our belongings across the porch up through the double doors into the Ferry.

Someone had been inside before us to turn off the alarm, but many of the windows were still boarded up and there were blankets spread over the furniture.

"Better wake the Old Boy," John said as we advanced into the sitting room. Triumphantly, he tore off the stocking cap that someone had pulled over the bust of Frederick Scheffield, a great benefactor of Gales Ferry. "Well, Scheffy," he drawled, patting him on the top of the head, "we're back!"

"Biglow," I said, flicking the light switches experimentally, "none of these lights works. We'd better hope that one of the freshmen is an electrician."

"At least the record player has a crank," he replied. "Have you ever tried getting this thing to work?" He indicated the battered Victrola in the corner.

I shrugged. "Bataillard's bringing his stereo." I picked up one of the old race programs from the pile on the edge of one of the church pews. Before 1970 the programs had been about the size of *The New Yorker,* but since then they had become smaller. For a couple of years in the mid-seventies, even the team picture had been changed. In the program from 1975, the picture was of the whole squad rather than the varsity eight. Sporting long hair, wearing sweat shirts and uncertain smiles, the Yale eight sat and kneeled below the traditional photograph of the Harvard varsity. With a glance at the two photographs, you could predict who won.

We returned to the main room, where I began to reassemble the Ping-Pong table. We live in squalor, I mused: bare light bulbs, a three-legged Ping-Pong table, old race programs all lying about. At least it is well-loved squalor.

"Damn!" came Biglow's voice from behind the piano. "Ever tried playing with a flat croquet ball?" He rose, holding between his thumb and forefinger a wooden ball which mold had reduced to the consistency of fudge. "What a dump!"

The varsity quarters are on the second floor, so John and I lugged our few belongings up the creaking stairs and into the long hallway. The hallway is lined with eight doors on a side leading into bedrooms. Eric, our captain, must have been there before us because there was a slip of paper on each door indicating who was to live inside. By request John and I were to share a room toward the far end. It was the same room Dave Potter and I had shared the year before, one of the few rooms with a view up the river toward Norwich.

The room was as I had left it. Thucydides was lying still unread on my bed. The Kaopectate was on the dresser. The dark dry panels into which we had scratched our names were as untouched as they had been for the last fifty years. In fact, with the exception of a few new pieces of Sheetrock to give the illusion of fireproofing, there had been no change in the room since the first oarsmen scratched their own names on the wall.

John ran his finger through the dust on the writing table, turned abruptly and disappeared down the hall. I flopped down on one of the mattresses and stretched out. These were regulation Yale mattresses that we had pilfered from the football team. They were seven feet long and barely three feet wide. No sheet fit them but even the tallest oarsman did not hang over the end. We had enough space in the room to dismantle our bunk beds, but that meant that the clothes on the line dripped on both our beds rather than just the top bunk.

When John returned he carried a bucket of water and two rags. The dust did not bother me, but it bothered John so much that he thought I should help him clean it up. John was the sort of person who arranged the pencils in his desk from shortest to longest. When I bought him a Dymo labeler for Christmas, he followed me around, leaving labels in my path. THROW Q TIPS AWAY, he put on the mirror. KEEP TOILET PAPER OUT OF THE SINK.

· Two seniors in the varsity boat would share the room next to ours. Ted and Andy had lived together for three years at Yale. For their last month rooming together and their last time at the Ferry, they would bring comfort with them. The bare studs along the walls would be hung with banners and pictures. The floor would be covered with the Oriental rug from their living room on campus. As juniors we had no need for such foofarah. We would be coming back.

After strewing my belongings about the room to show that it was occupied, I left John to his methodical un-packing and walked out onto the balcony at the very end of the hallway. The balcony affords a panoramic view of the river from Norwich on one side of the promontory to the bridge and New London on the other. The promontory itself was now barren, but before the fire it had been dominated by a small white house for the coaches. The rumor circulates that members of the local fire department broke into the house to drink and accidentally set the blaze. The firemen were also on strike. Secure in the knowledge that their strike demands would have to be met now that the dangers of an unemployed fire department had been demonstrated, the firemen staggered home. Anyway, no real harm had been done. The rich kids from Yale seemed to enjoy making themselves uncomfortable.

To the left of the promontory is the boathouse, a two-story hangar on pilings which provides storage for the shells and housing upstairs. The freshmen once lived in the upstairs barracks, but after the coaches' house burned, the fire department declared the boathouse unsafe—from whom, it did not specify. Now only the cooks, boatman, and trainer live there. Freshmen inhabit the large room at the other end of the varsity hallway.

Not more than half a mile downstream from the blue spire of our boathouse is the crimson spire of Red Top, the Harvard equivalent to Gales Ferry. Their dilapidated array of barnlike structures are tastefully set back out of sight in the trees. All we saw was the crimson beacon of their boathouse—scarcely visible but haunting.

From the lookout post of Gales Ferry underneath our enormous blue flag I gazed along the river to the camp of our enemy underneath their red flag. We had roughly identical facilities: the same shells, launches and oars. We had the same backgrounds and the same goals. The only significant difference was that their equipment was painted red and our equipment was painted blue. For a moment it all seemed silly, like something out of a Bugs Bunny–Yosemite Sam cartoon, but I then remembered the fund-raising dinner in New York when an Old Blue had drawn me aside to tell me that winning the race would be worth hundreds of thousands of dollars. I had thought that he would remind me of the rumor that victory would generate millions in alumni contributions to Yale, but that was not his pitch. No, the Race would mean hundreds of thousands of dollars to

me, just as it had for him, because it would give me the
confidence to do anything. That's crazy, I had thought
to myself. The outcome of any race and especially one
so long and unpredictable as the Harvard Race could
hardly be said to predict one's future; still, the instincts
that made me stop at Grandma Biglow's, that made me
ignore the crew of 1907, and that made me ashamed of
the crews since 1963 all told me that he was right. After
a victory, I felt, I would be able to do anything. The
Race was life, a chance to prove myself to myself—to
prove that fate, fortune and God were on my side. All
that stood in the way was Harvard.

That was reason enough to hate them, but we also
had more immediate reason. About a half a mile downstream on the far side of the river a billboard-sized rock
overhung the river twenty strokes from the finish line.
Upon our arrival last year we had painted the customary
blue *Y* on the Rock, but had used latex paint. Harvard
then managed to peel the latex *Y* from the Rock and left
the blob of rubber on our dock. After our defeat by
Dartmouth, Harvard decorated the Rock with a green
D#1, to which we responded with a crimson *H#3*. Since
then the rock face had changed considerably, but was
at that time defaced with an *H*. Many hours would now
have to be spent returning the Rock to its natural shade
of blue. Careful watch would then be maintained to
prevent further vandalism.

Four years before, after Yale had been thrashed in
both the varsity and freshman races, the full Harvard
contingent had piled into launches for an assault on the
Rock. Their flotilla paraded past the strangely quiet
Gales Ferry and then across to the Rock, where, much
to their surprise, they met with no opposition. The Ferry
had seemed deserted, the Rock was deserted, but in their

enthusiasm Harvard didn't give these signs a second thought. They painted Harvard's colors in triumph, never bothering to look back across the river to the abandoned grounds of Red Top. When they did, they watched impotently as a band of Yalies solemnly lowered the crimson flag. Yale had lost a race but gained a tablecloth. While not much of a trade, it was better than no trade at all.

A blast of air horns from the arriving bus awakened me from my reveries. Almost immediately Eric, our captain, bounded up the stairs, carrying our new Yale flag. Together we lowered the old bedraggled banner and raised the new one. "First practice is in forty-five minutes," he declared, engulfing my hand in his. "Let's get psyched for this one and all of them. Those bastards won't know what hit them!" During that moment the good-natured gleam had left his eyes, but he then grinned and disappeared into the hallway.

Standing 6 feet 6 inches and 213 pounds, Eric was not quite the tallest man in the boat but probably the strongest. My girl friend thought that Eric was gorgeous, which made me think that the veins and sinews rippling through his fine bronzed skin were a bit overdone, but I must admit that his physique was amazing. In 1978 Eric had been easily the largest in the boat, but in 1979 that distinction fell on Matthew, the sophomore seven man. Matthew was 6 feet 7 and, when hanging on the chin-up bar, could place his size 17 shoes flat on the ground. Grasping the chin-up bar flat-footed was the official "Geek" test. Eric, like Matthew, was officially a Geek. Although only a junior, Eric was elected captain because (among other things) he was no prima donna like me nor was he eccentric like John. Eric, of hardworking midwestern stock, was a self-effacing, dutiful, modern Hercules. A double major with distinction in English and economics, he later entered the crypt of Skull and Bones. He led by example, continually testing himself, knowing that pride would force the rest of us to attempt the same.

Eric, John and me: classmates at Yale and a nucleus of the Yale varsity on the crew from 1978 to our graduation in 1980. The only one of the three I haven't introduced is me, Steve Kiesling, 6 feet 4 inches of displaced Californian. I grew up with the classics, radicalism, TM, Rolfing, divorce, hot tubs, parapsychology and sports cars. I became an oarsman. If I could have introduced myself better, I wouldn't have written this narrative.

I rowed in the four seat of the varsity eight. Eric was at five, and John was the stroke. An eight, like a four or a pair, is a sweep-oared boat. Each oarsman rows with a single 12½-foot-long oar. The even-numbered seats (two, four, six and stroke) row on the port (left) side, while the odd-numbered seats (bow, three, five and seven) row on the starboard side. Sophomore year John, Eric and I rowed at six, five and four; and freshman year we were four, five and six. While some oarsmen can row either side, the three of us do not. Until John moved to the stroke seat, the three of us battled for seats in the middle of the boat, the engine room. Now John was at stroke, Matthew Labine seven, Andy Messer six, Eric Stevens five, I four, Karl Zinnsmeister three, Joe Bouscaren two and Ted Jaroszewicz bow. The boat was arranged with the largest men in the middle toward the stern (toward the stroke seat) and the lighter men at the extremities.

Nineteen seventy-nine had been a year of unquestioned Yale supremacy. All of our major boats were undefeated: varsity, junior varsity, freshmen, light-weight varsity, women's varsity, all undefeated. The Yale men's crews had won nearly five hundred shirts at the Sprints and close to eight hundred for the season. The Harvard race was a full month away and, after all, we had beaten them convincingly over 2,000 meters. In high spirits we unloaded the shells from their trailer, bolted back on the riggers and returned up the stairs to change into rowing gear.

The Rig

Tony Johnson, our coach, was bent over the varsity shell checking the adjustment of the outriggers when we returned. He seemed so relaxed as he moved from seat to seat down the boat, so completely different from the way he looked before the Eastern Championships. Only two nights before, his face had been grave but with just a touch of lightheartedness to give us confidence as he outlined our race strategy. The nine of us in the varsity boat had clustered around him in the hotel room, nervously wolfing down Oreo cookies until Ted got sick. The following morning Tony showed the strain. He huddled over the boat checking and double-checking the heights of the outriggers and the pitch of the oarlocks. It was too late for us to change any imperfections in the way we rowed, but there were subtle changes that could still be made to the boat. If the water was rough he could have raised the outriggers to give us room to clear the waves. If there had been a change from the headwind to a tailwind, he could have readjusted the oars to take advantage of the added push. There were other adjustments to be made, most of which we never knew about, but soon there was nothing left for him to do but give us each a handshake and a brief word before we paddled out to the finals. Tears streamed down his face when we returned to the dock to receive the last of the trophies.

Tony Johnson was known as Tony to everyone (including all but one of his four children, who inexplicably called him Dad, and John Biglow, who for reasons known only to himself called him Mr. Tony).

"Mr. Tony," John would say before each practice, "Mr. Tony, what are we going to do today?"

"We're going to work hard, John," Tony would answer soothingly.

"Does that mean that you're going to work hard too, Mr. Tony?"

"No, John," Tony would answer, "I'll ride in the launch."

The stroke of the varsity boat was very influential with the rest of the crew and soon several others began to call him by the same name. Mr. Tony was a very patient man.

Tony had rowed in high school, at Syracuse University and at Vesper and Potomac boat clubs. He supported himself by doing odd jobs so that he could row until 1969, when he became the head coach at Yale. Between leaving college and coming to Yale, Tony rowed in two Olympics and won two European championships as well as a handful of national championships. My most vivid image of Tony was one from a film clip that I heard about but never saw. The image was of Tony crossing the finish line in his pair, a two-man boat, in the 1968 Olympics. In 1967 and later in 1969 Tony and his partner won the European championships (then essentially the world championships), but as they crossed the line in Mexico City they raised their hands in victory only to discover that the East German pair had beaten them by inches. How it must have hurt, a silver medal in the Olympics.

When Tony accepted the head coaching position at Yale there were still the facilities and traditions that made possible Yale's 1924 and 1956 Olympic gold medal eights, but few oarsmen. Unrest during the sixties hit Yale hard and the Yale crew even harder—a time when Skull and Bones was on the verge of becoming a day-care center was no time to join the crew. By 1974 eight rowers and a coxswain were all that was left of the heavyweight crew; unfortunately, while the Yale crew deteriorated, the Harvard crew, coached by Harry Parker, got better every year. Nineteen sixty-three was both the beginning of the losing streak and the year Harry took over the Harvard varsity.

I then knew of Harry only as the presence that would soon arrive with his crew at Red Top. Three times I had shaken hands with him after races, twice in victory and once in defeat, but I had formed no impression of the man, only of the presence. Harry was the man who changed college rowing from a sport that began in March and ended in June to a sport that began in September and ended in August, with double practices during vacations. Harry was not patient with himself, with his oarsmen or with anyone else, but his boats won championship after championship and he then beat his own oarsmen in sculling, cross-country skiing and golf. In 1960 Harry was the U.S. single sculler in the Olympics. In 1979 Harry was thirty-nine, divorced, and living alone in a small apartment at the Harvard Varsity Club. Other coaches speak of the "magic" of Harry Parker that kept his crews winning year after year. Tony did not believe in magic.

When Tony finished checking the eight he surprised us by announcing that he would split us up into two-man boats, or pairs, for that practice. Tony was worried that the Sprints had dulled our concentration. Despite our victory, there were a number of small problems for us to work on—problems that could be ignored for a 2,000-meter sprint, but which might be critical over four miles. In a boat as large as the eight, it was often difficult to detect and isolate small problems because everyone compensated for one another. The smaller the boat, the easier it was to isolate the problem. Technical difficulties that went uncorrected in eights were embarrassingly obvious in pairs.

Enthusiastically Eric and I trotted into the boathouse to have first choice of the pairs. Yale's eight-oared shells were made of fiber glass or carbon fiber plastic, but the pairs were older and still made of wood. We ran our hands over their hulls, feeling for cracks or blemishes, and settled on an ancient but lovely shell built by George Pocock in Seattle. It was not as light or as fast as one of the newer plastic boats, but unlike the plastic boats, the Pocock shells never seemed to age. Our boatman, Jerry Romano, had built boats back in the forties with the elder Pocock. Jerry no longer built boats, but periodically he stripped the old boats and magically made them new again. Jerry's father had worked in the Yale boathouse and his son was learning the trade. Oarsmen and coaches came and went, but the Romanos always made sure that the boats were ready.

I felt a rush of excitement carrying a boat out of the boathouse and into the sunshine. It was an awakening, a birth. Oarsmen can and do make all sorts of jokes about shell-shaped objects and boat bays (not to mention oars and oarlocks and whatever one wants to make of the water). The symbols are there and must contribute to the profound satisfaction of the sport. Once outside the boathouse, however, I began to get nervous. There was a stiff breeze and rough water and it had been a very long time since I had rowed a pair.

The problem of climbing into a shell is difficult to visualize until you are confronted by one floating expectantly at the edge of a dock. An eight, which is about 60 feet long and only 25 inches wide, seems like a barge next to a pair. Obviously the pair's most natural configuration is upside down. Protruding from each side of the pair is a tubular steel outrigger which supports the oarlock. Prior to sitting in the shell one has to open the gate on the top of the lock and slide in an oar until the collar on the oar meshes with the oarlock. With the gates closed over the oars the boat becomes stable.

My problem was to achieve that initial stability with the rigger on the far side of the boat from the dock. A boat as large as an eight is quite stable. By bracing the opposite riggers against the dock it is possible to place one foot in the middle of the boat, lean out and open the oarlock. In a pair, however, the technique is not so obvious as are the consequences of failure. Looking out at the rigger, I remembered how I had felt mounting a horse for the first time. As a child of five I could barely comprehend riding an animal so large, but I was too proud or frightened to object. I feigned confidence. The horse, I figured, undoubtedly knew what he was for, and if he knew that I knew what he was for, all would

39

be well; even so, I succumbed to the irrepressible need to remind him of his purpose. "Don't move," I implored. "Don't do anything!" I leaped, the horse spooked, and I was once again on the ground—although not in the same configuration. I remember how the horse had regarded me. His eyes urged me to try again with the same innocence I have since encountered in carnival hawkers. The pair eyed me similarly.

I lay spread-eagle on the dock as if on the edge of a precipice and inched over the boat toward the lock. The lock, I discovered, was jammed and at arm's length I had no leverage to pry it open. I continued to pry without heeding the sound of a passing outboard. The gates were in fact easy to open when turned in the proper direction. I realized my mistake but not before the wake from the launch broke over the rigger. Thus baptized, I worked myself to safety in time to watch members of the junior varsity standing carelessly in their eight, placing their oars. "Go to hell!" I explained conversationally to no one in particular. By this time, however, there was an extra boatload of people on the dock. They too were baptized as the partially rotted dock sank under the additional weight.

Inside the shell adjacent to each rigger is a roughly bottom-shaped wooden seat that rolls on small wheels along two parallel steel tracks down as the "slide." Bored into each seat are two 1½-inch holes provided for one's pelvic bones. When I began rowing as a freshman, the holes had seemed too close together, but after a few months my pelvis conformed. There is no standard distance between holes. Oarsmen, I believe, develop a fluid joint in their pelvic girdles to adapt to varying seat configurations.

The two steel tracks of the slide are supported by a

wooden lattice suspended between the bulkheads, or "knees," of the shell and the thick wood along the gunwale. Also supported by the lattice is a 10-by-5-inch platform on which to stand while entering the boat. Older shells usually have the words "DO NOT STEP" stenciled into the hull to remind novices to step only onto the platform, but invariably some novice ignores the stencil and puts his foot through the bottom of the boat. The hull of a wooden racing shell is about a sixteenth of an inch thick.

Oarsmen's feet are tied into shoe-like devices called footstretchers. If their feet were not secured, they would drive themselves off the end of the slide and would have no way to pull themselves back. In older shells the feet are secured with wide leather straps like sandal straps and metal heel cups. Modern shells have real shoes screwed to the plate to make one's feet more comfortable, and one's life shorter should the shell ever capsize. The stretcher plate is mounted at about a 45-degree angle to the bottom of the hull. It can be shifted fore and aft depending on the length of the oarsman's legs; however, changing the position of the stretcher also changes the leverage angle through the oarlock. By moving the stretcher toward the stern, the oarsman is farther in front of the oarlock (the fulcrum), which necessitates a different stroke style than if the stretcher were toward the bow.

Tony believed that we should concentrate on our rowing and let him worry about the equipment. Eric and I adjusted the stretchers to what was comfortable and then tied our feet into the straps.

When visualizing a shell, keep in mind that the oarsmen are facing backward to the direction of travel. In the pair, I was in the bow seat and Eric was in the stroke seat. Eric's job was to maintain a steady rhythm, which I would then duplicate by watching his back and his oar blade. It was also my job to steer the boat, using the rudder connected by a loop of rope to my footstretcher. Swiveling my foot would turn the rudder, a process called "toeing." Generally we could navigate by keeping the stern of the boat in line with a known landmark, but occasionally I would have to glance over my shoulder to check for obstacles. "Blind boats," boats without coxswains to steer them, have a nasty habit of running into each other.

The design of an eight is similar to a pair but the increased size and speed necessitates a coxswain. In the Yale eight I rowed in the number four seat so I watched the back of the five man, who in turn followed six, who followed seven, who followed the stroke, who stared into the megaphone of the coxswain. (Modern coxswains often use an electronic microphone to communicate with the crew because it saves the coxswain's voice and makes his commands inaudible to the competition.) The coxswain is squeezed down into a seat suspended about an inch above the hull of the shell so that his weight helps stabilize the boat. He is the driver and strategist of the boat. He steers with a rope that runs from one side of the rudder along the top of the stern decking to the coxswain, where it loops back to the other side of the rudder. In older shells, the steering rope passed through wooden handles held by the coxswain. As well as steering the shells with the handles, coxswains clacked them against the gunwales in time with the stroke. Fortunately, coxswains no longer use clackers nor do they chant "Stroke" at every catch. Our coxswain called changes of stroke, coached, and coaxed us to greater efforts, but maintaining the rhythm was the job of the stroke oar.

When everything is properly adjusted and everyone is tied in comes the problem of rowing. As R. C. Lehman explains, "The problem broadly stated is to propel a certain kind of craft at its fastest possible pace through the water by movement of human bodies applying their weight and strengths by means of oars to this propulsion."

To understand the basic obstacles to rowing a boat, imagine that a spoked wheel stands vertically before you. Your task is to keep the wheel rotating by hitting the spokes with a stick. When the wheel is stopped or spinning slowly, the task is easy. Just place the stick between the spokes and push it along. But what happens when the wheel spins rapidly. If the stick gets caught in the spokes it will stop the wheel. To accelerate the wheel then you must hit the spokes with increased speed and energy.

Now imagine an even larger wheel, a gigantic wheel like the waterwheel at a millhouse, that takes up to eight people to keep it moving. Each inserts his heavy stick at just the right moment into the spokes of the wheel and pulls. If the timing of the catch of the stick in the spokes is not perfect, the wheel does not achieve its potential speed. If the timing of the release from the spokes is off, a stick may be caught in the spokes, transferring the force of the wheel through the stick into the belly of the hapless attendant—a graphic demonstration of what happens to an oarsman who fails to release his oar on time. This process, which has been known to catapult oarsmen into the river, is called "catching a crab."

While one is rowing, a more practical approach to the problem of placing an oar in the water is to imagine that the course is lined with a row of evenly spaced pegs on either side of the boat. To propel the boat, draw the body up the slide with the blade feathered flat to miss the pegs. Then with the arms fully extended and the legs cocked under the chest, square the blade and insert it behind the next peg. The peg then is a second-order fulcrum for the lever of the oar. Pull against the oar by opening the back, driving the legs, and finally squeezing the arms into the body. At that point the boat has passed the peg. Push down on the handle to release the oar, feather, and slide back up for the next stroke.

At each catch a shock surges through the body as the oar takes hold. The legs, shoulders and lower back tighten and drive backward the instant the oar hits the water. The point at which the oar is inserted yields and recedes as the boat begins to move. From the catch and through the stroke the shell accelerates, slowing down on the recovery between strokes. When a boat swings, the variation in speed between the catch and the recovery sequence is slight; otherwise, it can seem as if one of the sticks were constantly fouling the spokes. The boat has to be started again with every stroke.

Development of the modern racing shell achieved respectability in 1829, when the first Oxford-Cambridge race began the metamorphosis of the skiff from a means of transport to an aristrocratic racing machine. Modern racing actually began in long barges among watermen on the Thames in 1716; but the gentlemen of the 1800's repudiated rowing's practical origins. The regattas established by the watermen foundered beside the races organized by the new and exclusive rowing clubs.

The boats of that first Oxford-Cambridge race carried

the weight of their ancestry. Like barges, they had planked hulls and heavy keels. Oarlocks were mounted directly onto the gunwales, necessitating a wide hull to provide leverage with the oar. Most importantly, the early shells had fixed seats. Only the arms and back propelled the oar. Rowing those first racing boats must have been much closer to the tedium that most people have experienced in rowboats. Present racing shells have few of the same characteristics.

In 1846, Oxford dramatically decreased not only the width and weight of their shell but the previous record on the Thames with the development of the outrigger. Within a year the rigger was standard. Then in 1856 Oxford claimed another advantage by dispensing with the heavy keel of the old boats, creating a smooth bottom, the beginning of the shell.

In 1852 the first Yale-Harvard race began American intercollegiate athletics and launched the United States into boat design. The first race, organized as a promotional event by a local lodge, was raced in six-man boats without coxswains over a three-mile course on Lake Winnepesaukee, New Hampshire. The Harvard Boat Club, wearing blue, defeated the Yale Boat Club in red, beginning the 127 year-old rivalry. Not until 1876 did the race become the annual four-mile event in New London. Initially, American boats copied the British just as the Harvard-Yale race copied Oxford and Cambridge. In 1870, however, Yale broke the collegiate tradition by integrating the legs into rowing. Yale oarsmen wearing greased leather trousers slid up and back on smooth wooden plates mounted where the tracks of the slide are today. According to legend, a successful Yale crew were known to grease their seats with oatmeal mush. Although rolling seats were invented in 1871, the greased seat remained popular for several years. The slow acceptance of rolling seats is perhaps puzzling until one tastes Yale's oatmeal.

With the advent of the sliding seat, both the sport of rowing and the nature of sport were changed. By integrating the legs and stomach with the back and arms, all of the major muscle groups were harnessed. As well as increasing the speed of the boats, the new seat increased the possible energy expenditure. Few sports if any so completely tap the potential energy of all the muscles. Even swimming events of comparable duration burn far fewer calories than rowing races. Rowing races does not deplete the energy of the body so completely as running a marathon, but neither does running directly tap the power of the upper body. If one wanted to lay waste to all the energy in the body in the shortest possible time, rowing would be the way to do it.

Runners and swimmers, like oarsmen, impose more work and endure more strain than most well-balanced people can imagine. I do not wish to make more than jesting normative comparisons between sports—what serious athlete would admit that there was a better sport than his own? However, if one is exhausted by jogging five miles, he can then extrapolate to an appreciation of what it takes to run hard for twenty-six. The same is true for swimming. It is possible to appreciate at least something of the physical exertion of most sports from one's own experience. That is less true of rowing. Rowing looks easy. It is a graceful, beautiful sport which few have ever tried and that burns energy nearly twice as fast as running. All because of the sliding seat.

Everyone is in some way familiar with transcendent or mystical moments of sport. During a football game on television, there are those infrequent magical instants when even the spectator anticipates the impossible catch—an increased awareness between mind and body that transcends not only the body but one's relation to time. The intensity of the moment for the spectator is, of course, nothing compared to that of the player. The intensity is a function of the level of one's concentration, exertion and commitment. Joggers, I am told, occasionally get something of the same sensation but nothing compared to that of a world champion marathon runner. Who would dedicate years to marathon training if the same rewards could be earned jogging around the block? For oarsmen, the sensation is different. While

For oarsmen, the sensation is different. While running, swimming or even participating in team sports one performs to his own limits, limits set by individual conditioning and determination. When exhausted, the individual decides to endure, change pace, walk or collapse. As part of an eight, however, one performs at the level of the crew. When every part of each body says stop, inexplicably the boat still continues. Individual limitations reassert themselves only when the race is over; only then is the body released from the tyranny of the shell and allowed to vomit, lose consciousness or gracefully expire. (The *Guinness Book of World Records* documents the fate of a Japanese crew who rowed a race at a cadence of more than 50 strokes per minute. Supposedly, two of the crew died on the dock and the others died soon afterward. They lost the race.) In rowing not only is the intensity of energy expenditure greater than that of other physical endeavors but the possibility for exertion can become greater. Ordinarily the limitation of a crew is its weakest member; however, at the moment of transcendence, which oarsmen refer to as swing, the limit of the crew is beyond the strongest.

The sliding seat created the possibility of swing by merging complete concentration with total exertion. To a non-oarsman and to oarsmen who have not thought about it, this seems hardly a crucial advance for mankind. One cannot imagine the fate of the Western world hanging on such an insignificant invention. But it did.

Historically the invention of the slide had nothing to do with oatmeal-crazed Yalies. Time and time again the hopelessly outnumbered Athenian navy outmaneuvered, outrowed and outfought the Persian fleet. To their success we owe the splendor of classical Greece and much of our own heritage. Recent scholarship helps account for Athens' victories. Pottery paintings depict Athenian oarsmen carrying leather pads to sit upon while rowing. Oarsmen in Athenian boats are pictured with their knees tucked under their chests and arms extended—the top of the slide! Persians, on the other hand, are depicted with their legs flat, rowing with only their arms and backs. Greek poetry further corroborates the difference between Greek and Persian rowing. As an oarsman I find it galling that the only athlete remembered from this period was Pheidippides the runner, who ran himself to death over twenty-six miles to report the Athenian victory over the Persians at Marathon. Thousands have since commemorated his feat; however, the Athenians would have killed him themselves if he had brought news of defeat. Without the oarsmen and the sliding seat, the Persians might not have been beaten and then no one would remember that first marathon. In fact we might speak Persian.

Changes in the shell since the reinvention of the sliding seat have been mostly in materials rather than structure. Until the past decade the balance of power was maintained; now, however, technology has reinstated

the arms race. Wood gave way to fiber glass, which gave
way to carbon fiber and Kevlar, a superlight plastic substance. Our carbon fiber "Carbocraft" created a sensation when unveiled at the Eastern Sprints in 1978. Oarsmen clustered about the sleek silver-and-black aerospace
design, trying to guess its weight. Rumors circulated that
it was 150 pounds rather than the 250 pounds of a fiber-
glass boat or the 300 of the traditional wooden shell, but
most of the rumors were started by Yalies. The boat was
at least thirty pounds lighter and a bit stiffer than any
of the competition, but saving thirty pounds when the
gross weight of the boat and oarsmen approached two
thousand pounds seemed hardly significant. Neverthe-
less, if the competition believed we had an advantage,
then we had one. Our victory prompted other schools
to order their own Carbocrafts; but I believe that on
that particular day with our new boat, new oars, new
racing shirts, an undefeated season and a slight headwind, we could have won dragging a battleship anchor.
The same attitude, of course, cost us the race to Dartmouth the next week. Harvard followed in 1979 by winning the San Diego Crew Classic in "an old borrowed
Pocock," the most traditional of wooden boats. Two facts
are clear. First, the new materials give increased durability and are easier to maintain. Secondly, recent crews
have broken the records set by the crews of ten or even
five years ago. More than that is difficult to say. The
lightest eight at the 1979 world championships was a
Russian shell made of wood. The Russians lost.

Carbon fiber oars are more definitely successful.
Twelve and a half feet of wood, even slender, beautifully
crafted wood, is considerably heavier than the same
length of carbon fiber plastic; and unlike the weight of
the boat, the weight of the oars is not static. The more

mass that swings against the forward motion of the boat on the recovery of each stroke, the more the boat will be "checked"; therefore, the few pounds saved on each oar are significant. Furthermore, a good oar must be true and stay true. If the angle, or "pitch," of the oar to the water is incorrect, the oar will dive or wash out. The present demand for wood makes it uneconomical to let the wood dry for two or three years before building oars, but oars made of relatively green wood have a tendency to change pitch in hot weather. Changes in temperature and humidity forced Cal Berkeley's crew to readjust the angle of their oarlocks between the morning and afternoon race. As they sat on the dock with their wrenches, they had more time to appreciate the flash of our carbon fiber blades as we disappeared down the course.

Well-crafted wooden oars do have a special joy that is unmatched by synthetics. The weight of the wood pulls the oar into the water at each catch. With carbon fiber there is a conscious lift. I have heard that the lift is more precise. Perhaps. Wood, however, is more an extension of the arm. The sinew of the wood blends easily with human sinew, which, albeit less precise, better maintains the organic unity of the shell. Anyway, wooden oars hang so much better over the mantel.

With synthetics I sensed a greater alienation between myself and my equipment. The different flex of the carbon fiber oar and the lighter weight of the boats altered the sensation of swing. The boats were potentially faster but less pleasant to row. I once believed that synthetics were destined to ruin the pleasure of rowing until I discovered that the underclassmen preferred the feel of the new boats and oars to the old. Swing is not dependent on particular equipment. If I was to buy a boat to exercise in, I would buy a wooden single with wooden blades. If I was planning to race, I would buy the lightest boat available.

Using molded plastic and a radical hull design, a man named Robinson cut another thirty or forty pounds from the shell; but although it seemed potentially faster, few would row it. The hulls were not rigid, the riggers flexed, the footstretchers bent, and the reverberations of the seat along the slides overpowered the coxswains' loudspeakers—not to mention the stops on the slides, which lacerated the legs, and the protrusions on the edge on the seats, which violated from behind. Referred to as the "Kitchen Appliance" because it resembled a Tupperware washtub, the nine-thousand-dollar shell sat in the boathouse like a prototype B-1 bomber. We bought the thing sight unseen because Harvard had one. Harvard bought theirs because it was lighter than our Carbocraft and for spite because Yale's freshman coach was the importing agent for Carbocrafts. Harry Parker, the Harvard coach, had squandered his money, but said nothing. Figuring that if Harry bought one then they must be good, Penn, Dartmouth, Yale, Georgetown and God knows who else ordered them. Eventually, Penn's boat broke in half, Harvard's was rumored to have been lost under the frozen Charles, and Dartmouth's was rowed by their freshmen lightweights with a "For Sale" sign on the bow. I don't know what became of Georgetown's. In such a crisis, Yale remembered Title IX. We gave it to the women's crew and bought another boat. After the women rowed it to a national championship, we took it back for further consideration. All that the women's victory proved is that the best crew in the nation would win no matter what the equipment.

A Mention of Plato

The scheduled workout in our pair that day and in the eight for the rest of the week was designed to ease us back into rowing long distances. Rather than do the short-interval training that primed us for sprinting 2,000 meters, we rowed long pieces at low cadences; but as the rating dropped, so did our concentration. Where before we had rowed sharply for two or three minutes, we now floundered about for ten. The interminable miles seemed destined only to transfer more of the brackish river into the boat.

Tired and angry, we hauled the boat out of the water, rinsed off the slime and headed for the showers. Up to that point I had either forgotten or repressed my memories of the plumbing at the Ferry, but unavoidably they were restored. Here the quaint and traditional showed its other face. Descending into the basement, we sloshed across the hallway (which serves primarily to course the shower overflow away from the kitchen) into the wash-room. In the center of the cracked concrete floor stood two rows of yellowed porcelain basins drowned beneath warning signs against drinking the water. Back against the near wall were three ancient commodes, abused and abusive, which had been known to send the squeamish for the ten-minute walk into town. Finally there were four battered shower heads that dribbled lukewarm gray water intermittently onto the oarsmen crowded beneath. A bitter testimonial to the efficacy of the crew cut.

At least the evening promised to be good. I donned a coat and tie, sauntered into the dining room and tripped over a chair. The room had been rearranged! Previously the varsity squad had a separate table for each boat and the freshmen had been shoved off in a corner. The freshmen were still in the corner, but the other tables had been pulled together into a single large rectangle. I glared at one of the freshmen who was dis-tributing napkins. "What's all this?" I demanded, indi-cating the central table.

"The Senior Rules Committee told us to change it. Tony thought it was a good idea."

"Unprecedented!" came Biglow's voice from behind me.

"Unprecedented!" I agreed, following the tradition of all upperclassmen confronted by change. The fresh-men did not know that Tony had separated the tables only the year before. When those freshmen became sophomores, they would appreciate how traditions, es-pecially "traditional" duties of freshmen, changed from year to year, according to the whims of the Senior Rules Committee.

The year before, Tony had separated the tables be-cause of friction between the varsity and the less successful junior varsity. Separate tables were to increase the unity of each boat (and to contain the discontent of the junior varsity), a practice which ignored that the eights had been together for two months and that we had lived in close quarters on and off over the previous two years. The last thing we needed was more time with each other. Now that both crews were undefeated, the tables could be pushed together. I don't know if that was the stated reason for the change, but even at meals one had to earn his seat.

At the turn of the century a diet of porridge was thought to be the best way to make an oarsman tough. Fortunately, those good old days were over and the kitchen downstairs was stocked with enough food to have gotten Napoleon out of Russia. To prepare the feasts, most of the staff of one of the Yale dining halls moved out to the Ferry. When they cooked for four hundred, meals were only tolerably good; when they cooked for forty, however, the food was often impressive. Fresh salad and soup were followed by roast beef, beans and mashed potatoes. I remembered the five pounds that I had gained the previous year and denied myself a third helping. The denial was an easy victory, but I knew that as the month wore on, the third helping would exist only to pass the moments between the second and the fourth.

As I ate I glanced around at the coxswains to see if they too were eating. One measure of a coxswain's dedication was the amount of weight he would lose before a race because his food added weight to the boat. Coxswains too had to hurt, although no one ever put it in quite those terms.

My freshman year, Andy Fisher, who was 5 feet 9 inches tall and who looked emaciated at his normal 130 pounds, dieted to under 100 pounds for the race. From day to day he became skinnier and more taciturn. Even in the sunshine he wore sweaters for fear of catching what could have been a fatal cold. As a coxswain he was exempted from all chores but one, serving meals. Moving slowly to preserve his strength, Andy carried our plates and then joined the varsity table with his celery sticks. The varsity then had no chance of winning, yet Andy persisted as if sheer willpower would win the race. In 1979, after Yale found a couple of 80-pound women to cox, the Ivy League set a minimum weight at 120 pounds. Andy could now eat more normally and no one would ever question his dedication.

Dinner over, it was time for the annual haranguing of the freshmen. Amid a drum roll of spoons on the table, Ted, the bowman of the varsity and member of the Senior Rules Committee, pushed himself back from the table to begin the official welcome to the Ferry.

"Newcomers!" he began, amid cheers from the varsity. "You must by now know each other and all of us, but along the wall you will have noticed the faces of those that have come before you." With those words Ted gave a wide sweep with his arm, indicating the solemn rows of photographs gazing upon us. "Up there is Biglow's granddad, Jomo's dad, and Mikey's dad and granddad. God willing, we will all be up along this wall in the future; but for now all you newcomers must introduce yourself to the pictures, so stand up.

"Newcomers," he repeated solemnly, "state your full name (including your middle name and juniors and that sort of thing), birthplace, where you prepped, and sing your alma mater!"

And down the table went the list. Each freshman stood up, recited, sang and with luck was applauded into silence before he had finished more than a line or two of his alma mater. Those who balked were made to sing longer while those who sang with too much enthusiasm were applauded almost before they could begin. Afterward, though, it was the unanimous conclusion of the varsity that the "freesh" had showed too little enthusiasm. Their punishment was to clean up after dinner. In Dink Stover's day the team probably took the introductions seriously, but now it was done to give the freshmen a duty to fail so that we could make them clean up after dinner. Tony told me that was why such traditions were started in the first place.

To introduce officially the purpose of the Ferry, Eric read from the captain's log. As usual the reading dated from 1962, an account of the last crew to beat Harvard. I suppose the freshmen thought it an inspiring narrative, just as I had the first time that I had heard it, but having listened to the same piece for three years, I found it more than a little depressing. I drifted back to my room, once again caught in the fantasy of being included in the next year's reading.

The following morning began the routine that was to carry us through the month. It had been cold, raining and dark when I heard Tony's familiar morning greeting.

"Get ready to take your pulses!" Tony called down the corridor.

Through the wall I heard Karl and Mcgruder beginning to move. Even so early in the morning Karl was ready to rhapsodize. "I wake to sleep and take my waking slow," he intoned as Tony walked by.

"What's that shit?" scolded Mcgruder.

"Theodore Roethke, a slight bastardization."

Mcgruder, true to form, simply belched.

Meanwhile, Tony continued down the hallway,

pounding on doors and shaking beds till everyone showed some semblance of life. "Pulses!" came the call, and we dutifully sank back into our beds with our finger pressed against our necks counting the beats to see if our pulses were higher than normal—perhaps they would show that we were too tired to work hard. Seven beats and ten seconds later, I knew we would be working very hard.

Hearing drops against the windows, I dolefully pulled the pillow over my face, but as I did so, I noticed a flash of light. Instantly, I was up and scanning the horizon. "Did you see that?" I asked John.

"What?"

"Lightning, I think," I answered hopefully.

"That was the floodlight on the stairs."

I knew better, but the thought was always there: the hope that something completely beyond our control should intervene and prohibit us from practicing. More than one rest day a week would leave us worrying whether Harvard was also resting, but lightning was another matter. Tony, meanwhile, had become impatient. I reconsidered. No amount of cajoling could make someone work as hard as an oarsman without getting paid for it: therefore, I really must want to row. Tony was only facilitating my own wishes by waking me before dawn to row till exhaustion in the rain. Biglow was not amused by my epiphany so we again scanned the horizon for lightning. Nature not obliging, we rolled, groaning, out of bed, donned rowing shorts and headed down the steps to the boathouse.

Rowing in the morning, especially when it is raining, brings on more than just the obvious discomforts. I didn't bend well in the morning, but to stretch properly, I began from a position also conducive to agreeable tasks like sleeping. I lay on my back on the floor of the boat-house with my hands clasped behind my head and my legs together in preparation for the jackknife stretch, and with luck someone woke me before Tony noticed. And then there was the problem of digestion. Working back and forth on the slide early in the morning encouraged more than just movement of the boat, but once on the river, it was too late. One morning the boat became untenable, so we docked and ran for the nearest house. When the owner saw three of us at the door, he threatened to call the police.

The practice that morning was undistinguished, just long pieces at low stroke cadences. In my log I would write down the mileage, the stroke ratings and the drills that we had done. I would also write down anything interesting that happened. For the first few days we rowed about twelve miles a practice and rarely brought the stroke over 30. In my log I traced the development of a small boil that grew between me and my seat.

After a few more days of rowing long distances at a low cadence, we were ready for an appraisal of our progress, a four-mile time trial. It was another one of those windy, rainy mornings—the fourth in a row. By then the days of double practices and continual dampness were taking their toll. I woke up to discover that my last pair of dry rowing shorts had sat underneath a leak in the ceiling all night. No matter how good the trial could be, it would not be worth the additional boils of four miles in wet shorts. Angrily, I slithered into the sodden trou and went downstairs.

The air was gray and still as we paddled away from the boathouse, but soon the wind picked up. About half a mile from the bridge, waves began blowing over the gunwales. For several minutes we then had to wait until

Tony explained what sort of performance he expected and got the junior varsity set. I was dozing when Tony called for us to start.

Cold and sleepy, I was awakened by the spray. Waves crashed over the riggers, drenched us and slowly filled the boat. Even Andy's loudspeakers, which were mounted under the seats, slowly drowned. They were, of course, waterproof, but as the water had risen higher the sound had become muddled. A mile into the piece, there had been only a gurgle. By one and a half miles, silence. Above the wash, Andy's voice was a pitiful reminder of our own impotence. The coach's comment: "What the hell were you doing?" Tony never swears.

All of us, I discovered, had felt bad that morning. Unable to master ourselves, we had sought consolation in slugging it out with the river. The river always won, but we fooled ourselves by concentrating on how hard it was to row rather than on rowing hard. The galling fact was that if we had worked as hard as we imagined, it would have been exhilarating. As we paddled back to the dock, Eric suggested that we do an extra piece, so we turned the boat around and slogged through another thirty strokes before coming in for breakfast.

"We have three weeks to go and we are rowing like shit," came Eric's voice from behind me on the stairs.

"Yeah, but calling for extra pieces isn't going to help," I snapped back. "Whenever we have a bad practice, you just make it worse by suggesting extra work."

"We need extra work if we row like that. Harvard raced to the lighthouse; that's nine miles, and we can't even put four together."

"Harvard looked like they couldn't beat our JV when they passed us," I retorted.

It was an old argument, one that sprang up after bad

practices. Eric attributed poor performances to not enough work and would suggest extra pieces. I believed we worked too hard, that we concealed the fact that we were not moving the boat well by pushing ourselves to exhaustion. Rowing hard and rowing well were not necessarily the same thing, but without frequent races, it was difficult to tell which we were doing.

At that point Biglow squeezed between us and continued up the stairs without a word. Eric's gaze followed John to the top of the stairs and then fell to the floor. The year before, John had organized group encounter sessions. Unexpressed interpersonal tensions within the boat could slow us down, he explained, having just finished a course in group dynamics, so we had group sessions two or three hours each week in the manager's house. Since we lost the Race in 1978, no one ever mentioned reinstituting the therapy sessions, but it was not a good sign for John to be so quiet.

When the boats went well, the Ferry was congenial. Another row and yet another row, long rows, short rows, we lost all sense of time. Life flowed smoothly to the blades falling rhythmically into the river, but when we lost the rhythm of the oars, the pace of life was broken. We sank into ourselves, passing each other without comment, perpetually wondering if the month would be worthwhile.

At Yale rowing dispelled the tension of academic life. It cleansed our minds for other pursuits. But at the Ferry, there was nothing but rowing. The point of the Ferry was to be self-contained—the less contact with the outside world the better—and so long as the boats went well, the containment was pleasant. Then it did not matter what else was or was not being fulfilled. But we were more than just oarsmen. After a frustrating seminar at Yale I could row, but what could we do at the Ferry after a poor practice? Read Plato? And what if we should lose?

I remember waking up the morning after my first victory at the Eastern Championships in 1978. The night before, I had slung each of my fourteen new shirts on wire hangers and then twisted the hooks to catch in the molding at the edge of my bedroom ceiling. I awakened and sat up groggily under the last traces of champagne, thinking that it was time for practice, and then looked up at the wall and remembered. Victory in bright pastels flashed in the morning sun, and with that realization I was content to lie back and bask in the reflected glow. The night before Harvard I had gone to bed with just my Yale shirt and shorts suspended above the bed, hanging there in anticipation of the morning and the Race, and then the shirt was gone. I would wake up each succeeding morning with the weight—the weight that didn't fall until I sat up in bed and realized that it was over. It hit like a kick in the stomach and spread, but a kick would go away. After a few days the weight would lighten to a dull pain as life got under way again, but then we still had to face New Haven. On campus we had strutted, accepting our due as Eastern champions, who were as far as we were concerned the fastest, the best anywhere, all the way to the Race. Afterward there was always the question—at the pizza parlor, the barbershop, the dean's office, on the street: those simple two words from people who had not even heard the outcome, and who often didn't really care but were just trying to make conversation. "What happened?" And then I felt the weight.

During the hectic weeks before the Eastern Sprints we shuffled practices around final exams yet never had

61

a bad practice. Short, intense and precise. Our best rowing had been done when we were pressed for time. At Gales Ferry when practices went poorly, the suspicion returned that we would row faster with less time.

Following morning practice, we generally spent an hour at breakfast and then slept until lunch. Occasionally, Tony allowed us to return to New Haven for the day, but he disapproved of anything that might distract us from the Ferry. Even when we worked on our cars, Tony became anxious, ignoring that during the regular season we had looked after ourselves perfectly well. His insistence that we live and think within the confines of the camp intensified both our rowing and the pressures of the Race.

Having finished my morning nap, I walked downstairs, where six or seven oarsmen were hunched over the Risk game. Karl, wearing a leather World War I flying helmet, was romping through Afghanistan while Dave defended, wearing a surplus infantry helmet. Matthew had gotten himself stuck in Australia and even his red cap with gold wings could not fly him out. I knew his plight was desperate when he began commiserating with the rubber mouse that he carried in his pocket. Tony reclined on the sofa by the window, reading the paper and looking like everyone's father. I scouted the croquet course for signs of sanity. They were not to be found.

The croquet course appeared nothing more than the front lawn of the Ferry building, but lurking in the sporadically cropped grass were two stakes, nine wickets and the Act of God hole. As I watched, Joe was being trounced by Andy Fisher. I could see the frustration growing in Joe's eyes as he missed shot after shot.

"Fisher," Joe growled, "I know I am better than you

so your winning must be luck, so we are going to keep playing till I win. Otherwise, I'll get all gnarled up inside and I won't be able to eat lunch." With everyone so tightly wound that even a croquet game would leave someone mad as hell, I wondered what would happen once the real croquet tournament started. I hoped we would be speaking to one another by Race Day.

Second in prestige only to beating Harvard was winning the annual croquet tournament, a feat which, unlike beating Harvard, was impossible. The initial barriers to success were obvious. If one struck the ball ever so slightly in the wrong direction it careered into the lilacs or over the retaining wall toward the river. Either way, the loss of time was debilitating, although nothing compared to an act of God. If one's ball strayed into the hole, the immediate punishment was the loss of two turns; however, it was often more serious. After I contemptuously ignored the hole during my two previous times at the Ferry, it avenged itself by grabbing my foot as I crossed the course, carrying an armload of towels. The sprained ankle gave me an intriguing new pain to divert my worries from the Race.

Winning the croquet tournament was impossible because it was under the jurisdiction of the Ball and Mallet, a junior chosen by the Senior Rules Committee to organize the tournament and settle disputes. Being the sole arbiter, he could be completely arbitrary. One could never be sure that the rules, the court or even the object of the game would remain constant from one turn to the next. The Ball and Mallet had never been beaten and there was little hope for the future, but no one was discouraged from taking part. I felt confident. Biglow, my partner, was the B and M.

On the porch of the manager's house the self-styled

"Fascist Four" were preparing their strategy for the tournament. Mcgruder, Mike, Chris and Jim were easily recognizable in their blue Yale T-shirts, on the back of which they had stenciled "WASPS" in large white letters. These were the good old boys of the crew, Old Blues at twenty-one who in the tournament would resurrect the names "Plumbers" and "CREEPS." From them I borrowed *The Wall Street Journal* and learned about investment banks. Biglow, however, didn't get along with them well. I suspect it was their "Nuke the Whales" campaign in response to Biglow's Greenpeace porpoise pin that caused the final rift.

Lounging on the retaining wall with a sketchbook was Chris Choa, the French-Chinese New Yorker from Exeter wearing his blue silk smoking jacket and white scarf over a fluorescent orange bowling shirt. I could understand why the Fascist Four considered him a bit odd, but by his senior year his own blend of fanciful intellect and obsessive determination would propel him, tinsel-speckled scarf and all, into the bow seat of the varsity, the captaincy and the crypt of Bones. When Choa finished his drawing, we then walked to the local drugstore to see if the new *Sports Illustrated* had covered the Sprints. It had not yet arrived, but on the way back we stopped at the post office to collect the latest package from the film distributing company.

Gales Ferry did not have a television, but an alumnus owned a film distributing company and provided nightly movies. After dinner that night we sprawled about the main room, eating ice cream bars while watching the first reel of *Three Days of the Condor,* and then complained like four-year-olds when Tony said we had to go to bed.

The Test

Two weeks into the Ferry we had our next major test, a two-and-a-half-mile race against Navy. Like Dartmouth the previous year, Navy finished well behind us in the Sprints. We knew that we could beat them, but then we should have beaten Dartmouth. We were confident but subdued.

When the bus pulled up to the boathouse at Annapolis, the midshipmen were flying a Yale flag from one of their poles. They greeted us, congratulated us on the Sprints, and escorted us into the boathouse. It was flattering except for their paternalistic concern. Being patronized by oarsmen that we had clobbered only two weeks before was disturbing, especially because they had upset Harvard at a similar race the year before.

The following morning, the coddling continued. During the three-mile paddle to the starting line, they stationed boats to show us the way and gave rather too many people instructions to ensure that we arrived on time. Lulled into a new sense of security, we hardly noticed that the Navy eight was positioned nearly a length ahead of us at the start. The start was supposed to be staggered by one seat because of a slight turn in the course. A seat, not a length. When we pulled closer they politely but firmly told us to get back where we were. The right way, the wrong way and...I put the thought out of my mind.

Navy needed more than a length head start; in fact, after a half a mile the race was essentially over. In the first thirty strokes we pulled even and were beginning to pass when Andy warned of a wash from a passing launch. I felt the first rise as the bow hit the wake and then the rapid undulations, but we were prepared and flowed through the bad water without missing a stroke. Navy hit the wake like a deck of cards badly shuffled. Their six man failed to release his oar, transferring the momentum of the shell through the oar into his middle. Had his feet not been tied into the boat, he would have been catapulted into the estuary. Navy resumed rowing almost before the spray had settled, but the race was no longer a contest. They faded away like all the other crews we had raced to lose by eighteen seconds. "A horizon but not quite a time zone," we termed the margin in our new jargon for success. Navy resumed an obviously more strained patronage when we returned to the dock.

We did not get a real test until our second and final four-mile time trial the week after the Navy race. Knowing it would be the last indication of our chances against Harvard, we prepared for the trial as if it were the Race itself. We rested with light practices the day before and adjusted our schedule to row when the tide would be similar to Race Day's. The two lanes of the course had been staked along the river so we would not have to estimate the distance. It was not hard to convince ourselves that the real race had arrived.

Rested and psyched, we charged from the starting line striking a vigorous 42 strokes a minute, settled to 37 and then settled again to a solid 35. A mile into our race the junior varsity joined us for the last three miles. Although they began a little before we arrived at the three-mile mark, we surged past. At the two-mile mark the freshmen also joined the race to ensure that we were pressed until the finish. Again we moved past. In the last five hundred meters we raised the rating for the sprint and finished with the other boats lengths behind. If we rowed like that against Harvard, they would never even see us—or so I believed.

Tony did not say anything immediately after the practice, but called a meeting a few hours later. The sun was bright as we gathered on the porch of the manager's house. The rain that had been with us all week had lifted. All indicators pointed toward success. As we waited for his arrival I imagined the brief advice he would give us. Tony invariably recited the same parables before each race, and I knew most of them thoroughly. He would congratulate us on our performance, tell us to enjoy our day off and close with his favorite story, the story of limits. "There are no limits!" he would conclude at length, and then we would go back to the croquet tournament.

As I watched him come up the steps, I thought for a moment that someone close to him had died. The silver hair, which usually clashed with his youthful frame, made him look old. Clearly he was shaken as he gathered his thoughts. Then slowly, in what became a stunned silence, he explained that while we had rowed a high cadence, the boat was not moving well between strokes. There had not been much "spacing" between the puddles churned up by one stroke and the next. Contrary to what all of us felt, if we rowed as we had that day, we would lose.

A car drove by, the telephone rang, but still no one spoke. I lost myself in contemplation of a new blister and tried to think of a response. Never in my two years with Tony had he ever said anything so directly, believing that we should come to rely on our own judgments. All I knew about rowing was based on being able to trust what felt good. I had faith in my instincts, the faith of an undefeated season, but was it his record or ours? Tony had never beaten Harvard over four miles. For eight years his boats had lost to Harvard at every encounter until we had broken the streak at the Sprints in 1978. Maybe he thought us overconfident, but even if what he said was true, was it right to shake that confidence? We had the strength, the conditioning and the skill to win; that much I knew, but four miles was a long race, a lot of time to face the pain. Relaxation between strokes made the four miles possible, but relaxation was earned by confidence. Harvard's oarsmen could put their faith in Harry Parker knowing that his boats had never lost. They could just do what he told them and expect to win.

For the first time I felt afraid—knowing that fear would kill us. I wanted Tony to know what he had done, yet concealed my own weakness. What would the sophomores feel if they saw the tears forming?

I slunk back to my room to think it over. We had done our best and been told that it was not good enough. Not only was it not good enough, but the criteria for determining what was good had changed. I never checked to see if the spacing was good. I was not sure how to tell. The boat felt good and we had beaten the other two boats: what more could we have done? But if Tony said we were going to lose, then I supposed we were going to lose. No, that was impossible!

For the next few practices, I willed the spacing to improve, but the boat felt the same—and that felt good. After a couple of days Tony declared that the spacing had improved. I imagined that he just wanted us to stop worrying. In any case, I stopped thinking about it. I stopped thinking about much of anything.

The rain returned every day. I contemplated writing letters, but having nothing to say to anyone, I walked into the town of Gales Ferry for a new book. I did not find one, but I saw a few of the Harvard oarsmen. They refused to acknowledge my presence. The townspeople were rooting for us. They did not believe that we would win because so few of them remembered that we ever had won. They root for the underdog. I tried to explain to the postman that we were not the underdogs, that Harvard was expected to lose. He just laughed.

About four days before the Race, Andy Fisher tried to organize a coxswain's race. Traditionally on the day before the races, the coxswains from Yale and Harvard raced in four-oared shells from Gales Ferry to Red Top coxed by the heaviest oarsman from each side; however, because Harvard oarsmen shot water balloons at the Yale coxswains the previous year, Andy refused to race unless the race was switched to finish at Gales Ferry. Switching directions would have been a psychological coup, sixteen losses made any change advantageous, which was why Harvard wanted to maintain tradition. Later, Harvard agreed to the switch if their freshman coach, who had been a coxswain thirteen years before, could compete, but Andy thought it was only fair if both freshman coaches were allowed to compete (Mike Vespoli, our new freshman coach, had rowed in the world champion eight only five years before). I imagined that the Harvard coxswains would row to Gales Ferry while our coxswains rowed to Red Top. The two boatloads of coxswains would not even wave as they passed each other.

Unyielding pride and audacity make good coxswains. Through supreme confidence, coxswains coax oarsmen beyond what their own willpower can accomplish. Craziness, I had thought of their squabble over their race, but that same craziness would help us endure.

By Wednesday the Ferry was drawing to a close. Practices were mild and we were allowed to sleep late in the morning. The veils of exhaustion that had hung over us cleared more each day. Telegrams of encouragement became frequent and the atmosphere more festive. Time to put life in order before the Race.

For those weeks I had lived like a slob—a month spent in my own private locker room with clothes and towels strewn about the floor, kept damp and pungent by the daily rain. I had seldom shaved or even brushed my teeth. My hair, while short, was disheveled. Juxtaposed to the concentration and discipline of practice, disorder had been comforting, a mild rebellion to remind me I was no machine.

I picked the laundry off the floor, found my shaving kit and headed for the washroom. From the porch I looked toward Red Top and down the line of lane markers toward the bridge. The Race seemed for me and for the crew a rite of passage. Winning would establish the maturation of the new era of the Yale crew. Everything had to be in order so that we were free to focus. I considered writing my will and calling in my friends as witnesses.

Ted, our bowman, was completing his scrapbook, four years of newspaper clippings, started at a time when beating Navy was cause for celebration, to 1979, when we swept the championship. The scrapbook, a blue one with *Lux et Veritas* inscribed on the cover, began with an invitation to the freshman reception at President Brewster's house. By the end of the first year it remembered only the races. The graduation announcement that once centered the final page had been moved to make room for the Race program. Ted and the other seniors had graduated two weeks ago in New Haven. They were given a two-day leave to free themselves for the final gesture of their Yale careers. The scrapbook would help keep Ted's stories in line with the facts as we got older.

The final night, when John and I were preparing for sleep, Eric sauntered in and handed John a telegram from the captain of the 1963 crew. "FROM THE LAST CREW TO WIN AND THE FIRST CREW TO LOSE, SIXTEEN YEARS OF ANTICIPATION RIDES WITH YOU...GOOD LUCK."

"Thanks a lot," muttered Biglow. I read it and swore. We had been relaxed before reading the note. We needed to forget the burden of those sixteen years, yet it was in part those sixteen years that made the Race so important. As freshmen the three of us had helped break the string of fifteen freshman losses. As sophomores we had won the Sprints for the first time in twenty years, but we tried to forget the past. The last twenty years had nothing to do with the present; time and time again, however, we were told that it did. If we won, we earned that much more glory. If we didn't, nobody really thought it was possible anyway, but the task was clear.

I thought of Tony as he had stood at the head of the

banquet table after the previous loss to Harvard. He congratulated us on the season, on how proud he was of us and how much we had accomplished. His voice had been level, encouraging. It was a good race, he explained. We had learned a lot. "Next year..." he began calmly, but for an instant the calm broke. Tony drew himself up with a shiver and a newly formed tear. "But we've got to beat Harvard!"

That's his mania, his problem, I thought then. I was tired of being swept along as Tony's paintbrush, in a piece that we had been maneuvered into creating, but was not ours. Trying to do it for Tony or for all those alumni wasn't worth the devastation of defeat.

"Let's do it for Buzz!" The cry rang out for our freshman coach as we passed Harvard. For Buzz we did it freshman year, and for Tony we tried the next, but I realized now that we were not Tony's arms and legs in that race, or any race. Thrown together, with legs, arms, backs, breathing and eventually heartbeats in unison, we were physically and mentally one. Tony would be somewhere behind, silenced by Ivy League rules against coaching during a race and the knowledge that it was out of his hands. The mania, which had come to us as his, was ours.

How fast is Harvard? I wondered. The regular Harvard coxswain had failed to graduate and would not be in the race. Should we win, the alternate cox might become an excuse. I didn't care. Winning no matter what the excuse was preferable to losing. I imagined that Harvard would fall a length behind in the first couple of miles. After that, I didn't know. The previous year, I psyched myself, convinced that we would have to go beyond our capabilities, to row until we dropped and to keep rowing. Now I felt confident. With our best effort we would not be beaten. We had been pampered long enough. No regrets. I drifted into restless dreams.

Gunfire awakened the river. The Race was postponed. No, not postponed. Changed...horribly! We marched onto the bridge in rowing shorts and racing shirts, balancing on the guardrail. Every now and then the mist would part, and we could see our opponents, wearing crimson, similarly balanced on the opposite rail. Wind whipped around us, but where we stood was dead calm. Calm enough to load and aim our pistols. One shot each.

The mist was clearing. Occasionally I caught glimpses of the gallery on either bank. The survivors, wearing stained and faded shirts from past years, kept score. The gallery called to the coxswains, who called the shots. The two bowmen fired first, a muffled report and a dull thud. I wondered if Ted saw the smooth hole cut through his forehead before he disappeared, spinning end over end into the mist, but there was no time to worry about Ted. The splash of the bowmen was subsumed under the applause of the galleries. Every time the mist cleared two more shots rang out and two more scores were tallied. Ted, Joe, Matthew, Karl, John. The coxswain called their turns. Each raised his pistol, fired, and disappeared with a clean round hole drilled through his forehead.

How could a team win if no one missed? Only Eric and I were left to face the last of Harvard, and then Eric disappeared, taking with him the seventh of the Harvard eight. No one was going to win at all! Ridiculous! I raised my arm, sighting an inch above the barrel that returned my gaze, and pulled the trigger.

I awakened, struggling in waves of sheets. John was eyeing me curiously from across the room. Nauseated and in no mood to explain, I lurched into the bright sun on the balcony and looked up at our flag. A tailwind. Shit! The oath fell unconsciously. A headwind would have settled the boat, making our size and strength an overwhelming advantage—sealing their fate. The tailwind would favor Harvard. Perhaps the wind would change before dusk, but I doubted it. At least the Rock was still blue. Someone had been up all night protecting it. Already there were ten or twenty yachts at anchor near the finish line. Eric's parents were unpacking themselves from their car. The road must still be open. Eric's parents...A bit surprised, I looked down at my underwear and retreated.

All my belongings were packed. Thucydides had moved under the bottle of Kaopectate but was still unread. It would be over in eight hours as if it had never happened. The only loose ends were my racing shirt and shorts hanging above my bed.

All of us had slept fitfully. John looked whiter than usual as he climbed out of bed. "A tailwind," I told him, giving my voice no emphasis.

John shrugged. "Fast race then," and left. I wondered if it was taboo to mention such a disadvantage so soon before the Race. I had tried to keep all judgment out of my voice. Maybe it didn't matter.

After breakfast we paddled three miles down the course and left our boat at the Coast Guard Academy, one mile upstream from the bridge. We would launch that afternoon from the Academy because four miles was too far to row before the Race. The previous year we had left our boat and returned to the Ferry on board an alumnus' cabin cruiser, but the advice we were given during the ride left me so nervous I could barely stand. This time the van arrived to drive us back. The Harvard varsity would also launch from the Academy.

By noon the number of spectators was annoying. Those who visited were relatives, friends or former oarsmen, people who understood and believed in the Race, but each well-wisher meant an extra burden. We might hear them as we neared the finish, but they could not add to the Race itself. The Race would be rowed alone.

Rather than spend the day in worried anticipation, we piled into cars to see the local matinee. It passed the time. We returned to the Ferry in the late afternoon with only an hour left to brood. Most of the spectators had moved across the river or onto boats anchored at the finish. By that point I just felt tired. I remember that Joe walked into the main room, feigning the confidence that none of us felt.

"Gentlemen," he said, mimicking the voice of the starting judge, "my hand is down!"

Dread such as I had never felt before settled upon me. Normally those words brought a shiver of excitement, but now I wanted to leave, to sleep, to be sick.

An hour and a half before the Race, we packed ourselves back into the van and returned to the Coast Guard Academy. Tony had to be in a launch to help officiate at the freshman and junior varsity races so he could not be with us. He had called us together earlier but there had been nothing to say. I thought of Tony's two European championships and his Olympic silver medal. The pair he rowed had been the most successful U.S. pair before or since. Eight times he had watched his crews humiliated in New London. The obsession had grown every year, yet already this race was out of his hands.

The Harvard crew was clustered around a radio, listening to the broadcast of the freshman race, when we arrived. When it became apparent that our freshmen were well ahead I joined them. The mystique about Harvard was ending. Our freshmen had never witnessed the humiliation of a Yale boat losing to Harvard. Perhaps they would never have to. My own freshman year we had gone into the race scared to death. We trailed by a length over the two-mile course until the last few hundred meters when we began to close. We passed Harvard in the final strokes of the race, breaking the fifteen-year freshman losing streak. With our freshmen a length ahead three minutes into the race I felt better about our own chances. The tailwind was still blowing, but by then I too was only thinking of a faster race. If our freshmen could win in a tailwind, then we would have no problem.

Five minutes later the Harvard varsity was cheering. With half a mile to go their freshmen had moved back and were going to pass. I did not listen further. I guess we should have tried to instill a little more fear into our boat. While a freshman victory would have added to our confidence, their loss gave us something to avenge.

Another half hour of stretching and pacing, mostly pacing, and it was time to launch. Harvard on one side of the narrow dock and we on the other, our blades crossed in the middle. We had raced Harvard at the Sprints and passed each other numerous times on the river, but I had no real idea of what they looked like. They did not look that big. They did not look big at all. Maybe there was nothing to worry about. It was their turn to be frightened.

Then came disaster. Karl, our three man, had forgotten to replace a frayed shoelace on his footstretcher. I heard an oath and turned to watch as Karl stared blankly at broken string in his hand. The remainder was too short, and no one had brought a spare. After a moment's consternation our trainer, who was dockside to help us launch, contributed a lace from his own shoes. One thing always breaks before a big race. Better a shoe-lace than the oar Eric broke a few days ago. We shoved off, conscious that there was no one to sing the Yale cheer. I was glad. We were alone together.

As we had before our other races, we took a simple warm-up. A few drills, some long three-quarter pressure work, then a few "tens" and starts to get the cadence up. It was a warm-up appropriate for a crew about to row a 2,000-meter race but then so was our strategy. In 1978 we had tried to row down the course at a constant speed, relying on making up at the finish any seats which we allowed Harvard early in the Race. Slow and steady; but we lost by twelve seconds. Seats given up early proved impossible to regain after a couple of miles, so we intended to race now as if it were 2,000 meters. Go out fast, get a lead and hang on. Once in front, we could take control of the Race. If we were ahead after a couple of miles, no one would row through us. I kept thinking about the plan. Attack it! Get ahead in the first mile and commit yourself. So long as we did not fall behind early in the Race everything would be fine. Unlike other large races I was not mumbling "I quit" on every stroke. Neither was I rehearsing what to say to the reporters.

We rowed between the two pillars of the bridge to the starting line, believing that our entire season, indeed Yale rowing for many years, would be judged on the basis of our performance that day. We accepted the challenge. Where before I had been sluggish and stale, I was now powerful and relaxed, the excitement controlled and smooth. Confidently, we backed the stern of our shell into the waiting hands of the stake-boat boy.

Hundreds of feet above us, cars whisked by, oblivious to our drama. Up there were the shortcuts, the excuses, the world of infinite possibilities separating man and his potential. We had four miles and the best competition in the nation. We linked hands in a chain down the boat, committing ourselves to each other. I gave a final glance at Harvard, and then looked over my shoulder down the lines of stakes receding into the distance. We were set, the boats were aligned, and both coxswains' hands were down.

"Gentlemen! Both coxswains hands are down!"

"My hand is down!"

"Are you ready?...Ready all....Row!"

The blades locking in, backs opening, legs driving. The dull gray water began to boil. Three short strokes to get the boat in motion and twenty high. The cadence increasing with every catch. Remember to breathe and relax up the slide. Breathe and relax. Four miles. Start the rhythm one stroke at a time. Screw that, let's go! The stroke felt higher than usual but solid. Ten strokes gone—only ten more before we settle.

We had left the line at 45 strokes a minute, two strokes higher than in any other race in the season and three strokes over Harvard. Perhaps it was foolish to start so high, but as the commands were called, all the frustration of explaining for an entire year why we lost last time wound its final coil. The command "Row!" unleashed the desire of a year and nothing was going to stop it.

"Oh, you gods!" the Harvard five man had stood up in the shell and chanted to his crew in the shell after winning the San Diego Crew Classic two months before.

"I've got one Harvard god!" screamed Andy.

"I've got two gods! Three gods!"

The crimson blur beside us was dropping back. A seat down after ten strokes, three after fifteen. "Settle in two," yelled Andy. Four seats up.

"Settle!"

With an almost imperceptible hesitation returning up the slide, we dropped the cadence to 38. At the Sprints we had settled to 37. All I knew was that it seemed high but gloriously so. As we had moved to about a length up on Harvard, any doubts I had had about the Race faded. It was worthwhile after all.

I felt a wave of disappointment. The Race, it seemed, would be like any other that season. We would get a length lead early and then gradually pull away. A year's training had gone into these few races and we had won them all in the first few hundred meters. I wanted to win, but I expected more. I expected more until Harvard began pulling back.

In a four-mile race each stroke is at full pressure, but "full pressure" can have different intensities. The strategy for planning special moves during the long race can be critical. At a few hundred meters gone, Harvard took a "power ten" to move back through us. I heard their coxswain calling each stroke and saw their boat surge forward a seat or two, but all this was according to plan. Now it was five hundred meters gone and our turn to make a move. And move we did. We recaptured the distance and kept moving for the little orange ball on the tip of their bow. "I've got their bow deck and I want a bow ball!" screamed Andy, but Harvard held us.

Our cadence had slipped to a more sustainable 35 with Harvard a stroke or so below. The initial burst of adrenaline had been successful, giving us a lead and setting a vigorous pace which I didn't believe Harvard could maintain. I thought of the Sprints a month before.

We had been at the thousand-meter mark, halfway home and a length up on Harvard and the rest of the pack. At the thousand Harvard had taken a "twenty." I remembered watching, fascinated, as their stroke cadence came up a beat, and they started to move back. "Relax!" was all Andy yelled, drawing out the syllables in contempt, and Harvard's momentum stopped. I had looked upon Harvard with supreme pity and contempt. That move was all they had, I thought, and it wasn't good enough.

I now looked at Harvard with the same expectation. At some point we would see their last move and we would know it. In the meantime, the Race continued with Harvard taking tens to move, and us countering to regain any distance they made up. Harvard was not getting any closer but neither were they falling back. Our cadence was beginning to feel a bit frenetic. While the timing was good, we were not getting the proper relaxation between strokes. Andy, meanwhile, was not going to let Harvard forget that they were behind. As well as the microphone system which he used to communicate with us. he wore a megaphone for the benefit of the Harvard crew. Whenever we took a seat, Andy called it to Harvard's attention. If a Harvard man swiveled his head to see where we were, Andy exposed him. "The gods are looking!" Being in front, we did not have to turn our heads to see Harvard.

The bridge was not getting much smaller. It still loomed above, mocking our attempts to leave it. With a mile and a quarter gone, the end of a 2,000-meter race, our rating was still too high, and we were beginning to pay for it. Some of the smoothness had definitely left the stroke. I thought that we should drop the rate a beat or two but with Harvard so close I could not be sure.

Dropping the cadence properly could maintain the same speed at less cost. Done improperly, the boat would get sluggish. Andy had a marvelous feel for relaxing a stroke at just the right time. He had gotten us two Eastern Championships with the skill, so I resolved to let him worry about it. We had rowed the time trial at a high rating. On the other hand, Harvard had not been on our tail.

At a little more than two miles gone, our plan, so far as it went, had been successful, but I sensed trouble. We were in front as we expected, but Harvard showed no sign of fading. They continued to match us ten for ten; in fact, it seemed that they were taking more on their tens than we recovered with our own. As we passed the Groton submarine dry docks the water became rougher, threatening to throw off our timing. Relax, I kept saying to myself, but to relax took more concentration, more energy, than I had. The Harvard boat which had hugged fairly close to us had drifted well over to the far edge of their lane. With the boats so far apart it was hard to tell who was winning. I was afraid to turn my head in the rough water.

Somewhere in that stretch the boat tipped to starboard and I rolled up the slide and returned without ever setting my blade in the water. The boat balanced again, but during that brief absence of pain the unconscious rhythm had been broken. For a moment it seemed whether the oar was in the water or not made no difference, my legs did the same thing. In panic I rushed up for the next few strokes to prove that I was still there, still pulling. Harvard was clearly moving.

With two and a half miles gone, the boats were dead even. Each catch sent one boat ahead before the other boat took its own catch and moved back. We seesawed back and forth, stroke for stroke, with a mile and a half to go. There were occasional tens but there seemed no difference between moves and the base cadence. The boat hovered in an amorphous fog. My legs had lost all sensation yet my ears rang as if my body was screaming. I could not focus my eyes. Some magic kept my oar and body sychronized with the others, but to my knowledge I was just throwing myself back and forth. Harvard called another ten to move but made no progress. Through the mist that was filling my brain I could hear Andy taunt them, "Not hard enough, Harvard!"

Fury brought me back. Taunting a boat that was moving would make them move faster. Cursing my own prophecy, I heard Harvard's next move and saw them take the lead. I was breathing better and probably pulling harder, but when a boat moves past another after a struggle, triumph will keep it moving. Soon Harvard was a half a length ahead.

Andy was not saying anything so I did my own calculations. With less than a mile to go we were three-quarters of a length down. How much did I have left? At what point could we kick the rating up and sprint ahead? If the rating was called up I knew that I would stay with it; faith and three years of training would see to that. But I also realized that the decision to work harder was no longer mine. I could do more if Andy demanded it of the boat, but I was too exhausted to demand more of myself. I needed Andy to persuade me that I could.

The sound of the crowd from the spectators' yachts focused us as we neared the finish. "Eric, let's go!" I gasped forward, hoping to revive myself with the words. "Please, Andy, call it up." My voice probably had not carried even as far as Eric. I felt old and sluggish—the

Race had become slow motion. The ringing in my ears was now the sound of a bell on one of the launches. Harvard was eight seats up but still within range.

Andy called the rating up. Surprisingly, the boat surged forward. Eight seats down, now seven...six. So long as the surge continued, we were still in the Race. With twenty strokes to go a blade caught a little water, and the boat rocked to starboard. Nothing special, but we stopped gaining—five or six seats behind and ten strokes from the finish line.

I looked down to pick up my rowing clothes after showering, but my shirt was not there. I searched for several minutes before it occurred to me that the shirt now belonged to Charlie Altercruse, the Harvard four man. "No one can beat you guys over two thousand meters," he said, as I handed him my shirt. I smiled before I began to cry. We had given all we had. There were no regrets. Next year. The rest of our squad cheered as we returned to the Ferry.

The Release

Important to the execution of such tasks as rowing and long distance running is a high level of determination, the ability to ignore pain and other personality traits denoting persistence and durability. It is usually found that most individuals participating in these types of activities are introverted. They are usually stable emotionally and, in addition, exhibit sound physiological characteristics and good self control.

—VANEK AND CRATTY,
Psychology and the Superior Athlete

Introverted, with a stable disposition and a high tolerance for pain. But you don't start out with a high tolerance. It builds from day to day and year to year, from what seems to be the limit of physical endurance to what is the limit. Eventually, when I rowed, my legs lost all sensation. They went up and down, still pushing, but feeling nothing. My mind continued, oblivious to my body, returning only now and again to wonder if permanent damage was being done to the machinery that supported it.

That night I fled the Ferry. I fled the Race and the choruses of "Maybe next year." We had beaten the old course record by more than twelve seconds, a feat to be proud of, but now that it was over, I could feel nothing. In the Blue Room of the manager's house we reelected Eric captain, then in fulfillment of the tradition we raised our champagne glasses in salute and dashed them into the fireplace. Twice my glass bounced intact from the mantel. Twice denied. Two races, I thought, as I crushed the glass under my heel. Hours later, the junior varsity was still celebrating its victory; drinking, wrestling, spraying fire extinguishers, flooding the hallway as Andy drowned his rug with tears. Ted appeared asleep. John twitched in the bed above me, unable to sleep, yet refusing to talk. Quietly, I added my rowing shorts to the bags that I had packed the day before, shook John's hand and headed out into the night.

The bridge shimmered with distant headlights as I carried the last of my belongings to the car, but the fog was closing. As I finished loading, the bridge disappeared. Red Top disappeared. I awakened the cold, forgotten engine as the Ferry faded.

For an entire year we had anticipated that day, that race, and as it closed upon us we wished only that it be over. So much, maybe too much, had been at stake, and then to shave twelve seconds from the record and still be short by three—. The alumni could not help us for our pain was mirrored in their eyes. And we were of no help to each other. Each of us felt that he personally had propelled that boat into the lead and that his failure, my failure, had relinquished that lead. The night before, as John and I lay in our bunks, he confided that he did not think it possible for anyone to move a boat faster than he. I concurred. If there was anyone who could move a boat faster, it would be I. Afterward, John's eyes registered shock, disbelief and fear, as if he had betrayed both of us. We had been the best, we would not deny that, so we must have betrayed ourselves. As friends we could not face each other, but neither could we face each other as rivals. The duel seemed over, and we had both lost.

Alone, I fled to my lover in New Haven, hoping to resume life as I had left it a month before. As had most things in my life, Karen had conflicted with my concentration and been left behind. I had not been able to tolerate her encouragement and finally her love because she brought me outside of myself. Now what I needed most was to get outside myself.

Arnold Schwarzenegger, the champion body builder in the movie *Pumping Iron*, mentioned that he refused his mother's request to attend his father's funeral because it was too close to a major competition. The audience around me hissed, but they cheered when he won the contest. People left the theater reviling him for his unabashed narcissism while imitating his poses—sharing his victory while damning him for the obsessiveness that made him victorious. I wished that I had the same faith in rowing that Arnold had in body building. I felt I had done the same to Karen that Arnold had done to his mother, but unlike him I had lost.

Karen's room was yellow and gray beneath the cracked porcelain light fixture on the ceiling. The walls and shelves were barren and boxes blocked the door. Together we sat on the mattress on the floor, watching each other without knowing how to break the silence, or whether it should be broken. She had loved me for the clarity that marked my endeavors, the purposefulness with which I attacked rowing and wooed her. She had sustained me until rowing became sustenance enough.

Karen and I had first met on the dock at the boathouse as she carried her single scull down the gangway. Before coming to Yale, Karen had rowed for the Massachusetts Institute of Technology, a place where involvement with athletics was more important than success.

Karen rowed for what the venerable American shell builder George Pocock called "the symphony of motion." As dawn breaks over the river, the shell is lifted from its rack out into the morning. On another rack the oars hang ready to be greased and slipped into the locks. Then, awakened to the river and the feel of the oars, the oarsmen blend in fulfillment of the shell. The symphony is not of competition. It is the synchronous motion over water, the harmonic flexing of wood and muscle, where each piece of equipment and every oarsman is both essential to and the limit of motion itself. Complete autonomy within a perfect union.

The symphony of motion is the aesthetic of rowing. It is exhilaration, the flow of vitality which promises immortality yet soon leaves one exhausted and satisfied. The aesthetic exists in the present. While attained through hard work, the sensation defies the determination that makes it possible, a magical freedom made possible by the merging of man and machine. I believed that Karen achieved that feeling without competing. For me, however, rowing had become the means to winning races. The symphony had been interrupted by the din outside. I held out my hands but I could not look at Karen.

Freshman year my hands had been cut by the oar, opening blisters that made paddling excruciating. Gradually the pain went away. After three years, my hands were not only callused, but the long fingers seemed thicker. I once held my finger in a candle flame to test its toughness, watching as the skin began to blacken. The flame probed the finger in search of reaction until, bored with the interrogation, the finger dropped, smothering the flame in molten wax.

The top of my finger was discolored already. During the race, my blade hit a wave which in turn slammed my hand into the gunwale. There was no pain. The only trace of the incident was the blood under my crushed nail and a dull throb at each pulse.

I imagined that within me was a smaller person, the person who developed long before my muscles, who realized as I grew larger that he could not escape. To the inner self, the self that had always been, the outer body was expendable, capable of being abused beyond all its assumed limits. What mattered was the will, the integrity of what was inside.

Dominating this large frame numbed my senses, but what did Karen call it? Callousness, insensitivity? Through the years and up the athletic ladder, competition increased my willpower, self-confidence and strength of purpose, but what was the cost? Karen had been competitive but it was only a fragment of her life. At the cost of some time and a few blisters, she kept fit but was not overwhelmed. Being in shape was not my goal. My body was a tool to test the capabilities of my will.

My hands were laced with a network of testimonies to earlier competition. What struck me was that the scars were so recent. Not too many years before, when I hurt myself I quit. Now I tried to create and to endure more pain. Perhaps the long gash left over from high school football defined the change.

If it had been earned in a game I might not think much of it. The torn hand would in time have become a fond memory of high school glory. But it was no game. There was not even a team. The commands were called by the coach. I crouched on one side of the fifty-yard line and Randy on the other. The line coach, who had been unable to decide which one of us should be on the starting team, stood to one side. Randy had played his three previous years of high school but was uninspired. I too was a senior and slightly larger than Randy, but I had never worn pads until three weeks before. The coach thought it necessary to have an objective solution. Whoever knocked the other back over the line two out of three times would start that Saturday.

I had wanted to object. I had built myself since the previous winter with hopes of making the team, practicing desperately to make the meaningless strings of numbers become instinctive motions. While previously shy, I had rationalized the violence of the game, concentrating on the form of my tackles rather than the object. Randy had put in his years in the junior varsity knowing that as a senior he would be promoted; in fact, he had been guaranteed a spot on the starting lineup until I joined the team. Randy's three years of drudgery stood against my rationalizations.

"Right, fifty-two, set... Go!"

I slammed across the fifty-yard line into the opposing

tackle, but I had not lowered my shoulders and my helmet slid over Randy's as he hit my chest. Too late I swung one fist to deflect the blow, but the web of my hand merely hooked a loose rivet on his helmet and ripped free. I was driven back over the line.

Humiliated, I noticed blood streaming down my hand. The rivet tore a ragged gash from the web of my hand to my wrist which would need stitches, but would also end the contest. I would forfeit the battle, but it could not be said that I had been beaten; however, the coach did not notice my hand, and called us back to the line. Angered, I crouched lower and smashed squarely into Randy's helmet, recoiled, and knocked him backward. One to one. My fury abated, I returned for the third time and was clobbered before I completed a step.

The throbbing in my hand was almost unbearable as we awaited the return of the team, but rather than nurse the wound I encouraged the pain. Rationally I knew that it was my own failing that hurt me. I did not have the instinctive drive to play football, but it was too late to quit. Before, violence made me uncomfortable, but having lost, I forgot my discomfort. A few minutes later, when I was put on defense opposite Randy, I smeared blood across my shoulder pads and swore to hurt him so badly that he could not start on Saturday. My coach told me I was becoming a man. I soon became a first-string football player.

I thought of the blood as I reached for Karen. My hand seemed separate, foreign, almost evil—far too clumsy and coarse to be capable of love. Karen would not accept it, she would recoil. But then I felt something wrong in her touch. Its softness puzzled and then angered me.

From the feel of her hand, Karen could not have

attained the symphony. She could not have committed herself. Treating rowing as a peculiarly engaging pastime, how could she feel the same significance? How could she comfort me? Competition, *Com-petitio,* a questioning together, a striving together. Competition allows each participant to achieve a level of excellence that could not have been achieved alone. Otherwise, rowing did not transcend the individual. The problem was to find a balance—the balance between the often ruthless desire to succeed and the aesthetic. Before the Ferry we imagined each other as completing ourselves. That was not the answer.

Becoming

Sex, I had been told, is a sublimation of rowing, but, for that matter, so was everything else. Once one is beyond a certain level of commitment to the sport, life begins to seem an allegory of rowing rather than rowing an allegory of life. The instances in practice that had once been called upon to help illustrate the complexities of the outside world gradually began to seem more real and significant than what they were supposed to illustrate. I wondered what happened to the once conscientious philosophy student. I wondered why, instead of reading Hegel, I was pulling an oar through the water, repeating the same motion for the millionth time. Having left Hegel to fend for himself under a pile of racing shirts, the philosopher oarsman felt the tug of conscience. Why do it? I chose classes that would not interfere with practice. The Eastern Sprints dictated my exam schedule. I paid, or at least my father paid, eight thousand dollars a year for me to row. The least I can do is be able to tell him why.

Once one has attained a high level of success at any pursuit and especially an unorthodox pursuit like rowing, one develops a number of generally self-congratulatory half-truths to explain how it happened that he ascended to that particular pinnacle. Often because original motivations don't seem to have much in common with the eventual success, the real and rationalized motivations are difficult to separate.

While Yale has a large number of athletic teams and athletes, it is full of people who never made peace with athletics. Intellectual disdain for certain sports is widespread because so many students gained admission by devoting themselves to study. In high school an athletic image was worth striving for, but those who come to Yale as athletes find the academic welcome not always warm.

Yale emphasizes performance. It is a place where introductions follow the form, "This is Steve, he's on the crew." *Homo faber,* man the creator, except that the goal is to excel. When I came to Yale I believed that if I managed to excel there, I would be assured of excelling anywhere. The best in the tradition of the University was not the best by handicap, it was the best. If you graduated at the top of your class, you were assured of being at the top anywhere, but what if you were an athlete at Yale? The best football or basketball players don't go to Yale because it would compromise their talent, yet when Yale lowers its academic standards to encourage better athletes, then the compromise is both athletic and academic. If you are the sort that will not compromise, Yale football is not the answer.

Rowing does not necessitate a compromise or at least

not the same compromise. Most oarsmen at Yale had not rowed before entering college (only three oarsmen from the varsity eight had rowed before Yale), and those who had rowed previously were not given much extra consideration by the admission office. While many of our oarsmen had played other sports previously, several were new to athletic competition—people who spent most of high school explaining why they weren't playing football and decided to make peace with sports once the pressure was off. There is no academic compromise in admissions, yet successful Yale oarsmen were on their way to becoming world champions. The ideals and accomplishments of the rowing team seemed more in keeping with the spirit of the University than any other sport—at least that was what I told myself when I tried to justify spending so much time in a shell. As I think back, however, my own introduction to rowing was fairly haphazard.

I did not feel like Dink Stover riding in the dank Connecticut shuttle from Kennedy Airport to New Haven. My grand entrance to Yale had begun the night before on the Red Eye flight from San Francisco. Now, the Red Eye having worked its magic, my voyage was almost over. Tired and apprehensive, I tried to relax. I could see my reflection distorted in the rearview mirror so for lack of anything better, I contemplated it.

California had been beautiful, warm and sunny. Living there for eighteen years, I had managed a tan. I must have looked like a Californian with my polyester shirt, long sun-bleached hair and blue eyes. Not a southern California surfer but a long way from New Haven. Not like a Yalie, I suspected, but I did not know why. Once again I ran through my qualifications for being: "A" student, student body president, debater, football player (senior year), alumni preference. A onetime football player whose father had gone to Yale, the thought echoed through my mind. A chimpanzee could get into Yale with athletic and alumni preference. But could one survive? I wondered if the coaches knew that I had no intention of playing.

In the next seat were two upperclassmen, or at least what I took to be upperclassmen. They had boarded the limousine at different terminals yet greeted each other with the casual assurance of old friends. I supposed that they ought to have been friends for they were indistinguishable. Both were short with black curly hair, large noses and tortoiseshell glasses. They dressed like my father. Brooks Brothers combined so well with that strained emaciated look that I feared it was a prerequisite for good scholarship. I shifted about, trying to appear small, but my size seemed proof enough against any chance of serious academic pursuit. Imagining a scarlet football emblazoned on my chest, I reached into my pocket for my glasses. I had grown accustomed to contact lenses but they seemed out of place. Comforted by the impressive thickness of my own lenses, I ostentatiously uncovered my course catalog and flipped through the pages. A few days before, I had puffed up at the opportunity to inform someone casually that I was going to Yale. Now I felt an impostor.

In retrospect, I wonder how my conception of Yalies began. I had visited Yale the previous spring to visit my sister and to be interviewed. My sister was then a sophomore and a very serious student who has since gone off to Oxford to study ancient history. She was also a demonic oarsman. During my visit I don't remember meeting anyone who didn't row. Introductions consisted of explaining which seat of which boat the person rowed in. That information, it seemed, was sufficient to know anyone. I also discovered that oarsmen are very large. The majority of the men that I met were over six feet and the women were trying to be. Everyone told me that I had the perfect build to be an oarsman. Having been told the same thing about football in high school, I was leery but pleased. I still did not know what rowing was, but I left feeling obligated to try it.

My perfect rowing build was of little solace when I entered New Haven on the day before freshman registration. It had begun to drizzle and the city was shrouded in steam. By the time I had collected my bags and walked across the Green to the Old Campus, I was soaked. At eight in the morning, it was time for my daily bicycle circuit in the cool bright hills where I lived, near Stanford University. I longed for Stanford. Stanford itself is made of stone but it seems spacious and comfortable. In contrast, the stone of the Old Campus looked damp and dark, barely supporting the grim strands of ivy.

Sitting on my duffel bag in my barren room in Wright Hall, I pondered the next four years. My roommates had not arrived. I could not find my sister. My only company was an obviously unused broom and the remains of a candle on the mantel. From across the courtyard I thought I heard a stereo playing. I flung open the heavy leaded-glass windows in time to catch the last chorus of the Beach Boys singing "California Girls." I could have stayed at Stanford in the sunshine with my girl friend, but the mystique of the Ivy League had drawn me east.

Several hours later I slipped on my sandals and left in search of my advisor, a philosophy professor in the Divinity School named Franklin. I had no idea who he

96

was or what he could do for me, but the course book advised each freshman to pay homage to his advisor as soon as possible. Determined to make a good start at college, I ambled up beyond Science Hill to the Divinity School. On my way I noticed a copy of a treatise on C. S. Lewis written by my advisor in the window of the bookstore for three ninety-five. Thinking that an easy way to get on good terms with the man was to buy his book, I bought a copy and skimmed the first chapter as I walked.

Franklin was on the phone when I came into his office. He waved me to a chair. I had never been so near to a Yale professor before, so while appearing to look through my notebook I inspected him. He was younger than I expected, not past middle age, but his bulk gave a certain majesty. His speech was slow and dry. I had anticipated a priest but had found an attorney. At least his office fulfilled my expectations. It was small, dark and overflowing with books and papers. A crucifix hung crookedly behind the desk. After nearly ten minutes he hung up the phone, sat back and inspected me. I clasped my hands together to keep from fidgeting.

"Do you realize the trouble with Californians?" He waved a piece of paper airily. "They grow up without discipline." I realized that the paper was my application to Yale and tried to remember what I had written. Nothing incriminating, or at least I couldn't remember anything.

Franklin rose without taking his eyes off me. "I have known serious scholars who have gone to Berkeley and disappeared academically," he continued. "They were not willing to work. Are you willing to work?"

"Yes, sir," I whispered.

His voice became almost fatherly as he explained to

me the problems he had experienced with Californians in the past, something to do with the permissiveness of California's public schools. Of course, it was not really my fault, but I would have to work extra hard to adjust to Yale's rigid standards. My fear was turning to anger.

"Do you intend to devote your time to anything in particular outside of classes?"

"Yes, sir. I think I will row on the crew," I replied. "I understand that I have potential as an oarsman." Franklin remained impassive, but the choice seemed acceptable. He might have preferred something more academic, but at least I was siding with the right coastline.

"Do you have anything to say to me before you go?" He asked finally. I was still angry and could not tell if it showed. Perhaps I was being baited. He wanted to see what I would do under pressure. I could discern nothing from his manner.

"Yes, sir, I think your treatment of Lewis is peculiar," I stammered, holding his book. "Perhaps we can talk about it during my next appointment." He shook my hand as I made my escape. Later I was to sign my own schedule rather than discover whether his treatment of Lewis had indeed been peculiar.

Buying the book had saved me from being demoralized, but I was shaken. If the Divinity School could not be counted upon for fraternity, I was not anxious to meet the regular professors. I had also learned something that was both a relief and profoundly disturbing. At Yale, where excellence was at such a premium, one could get by with sheer bravado. In academics there were shortcuts just like almost everywhere else. I had often played the shortcuts although it seemed dishonest, like learning for the first time that there is no gold behind paper dollars. It was necessary, made life more interesting, but at the same time there is the vague (and sometimes not so vague) feeling that it all has no foundation. I had chosen Yale over Amherst College because I was tired of dividing my energies into several different pursuits. I looked to Yale to allow me to achieve some particular goal that no shortcut could earn for me. Trying to predict the fate of a tower, even an ivory tower, if it had a foundation of bullshit, I wandered through campus, gazing upward at the cold stone.

Still shaken, I wandered back to the middle of campus and sat down on the lawn above the underground library to watch two fellows playing catch with a Frisbee. They seemed too stiff to be enjoying the game, so I figured that I could enlighten them with the "California touch" if the Frisbee happened in my direction. Almost immediately, the Frisbee sailed over the nearest man's head and landed only a few feet away. The throw seemed intentional, so I took it as an invitation to join the game; within minutes, however, one of the two had to leave. The other invited me to sit with him while we awaited his friend.

"Where are you from?" he asked after a few moments.

"Portola Valley, California," I answered, happy to have anyone to talk to. "Right near Stanford University."

"That's interesting. I just recently met a guy from Stanford on a mission."

"A mission?" I asked dejectedly. The Frisbee had been thrown to me for a purpose.

"Yes, a chance to spread the light of Reverend Moon to a small French village."

"No shit?" I said, picking myself up. After a few steps I paused. The Moonie was smiling after me. Without another thought I began to run. Dejection led me into the arms of Buzz Congram, the freshman crew coach.

The Payne Whitney Gymnasium is fourteen stories tall and easily confused with a cathedral; in fact, it always seemed to me much more sacred a place than the Divinity School. I was standing by the entrance, investigating the stonework and wondering what sort of identification was necessary to enter, when Buzz appeared. I had met him only briefly the year before, but he recognized me and remembered my name. Although he was late for a meeting, he ushered me inside—into what seemed the very foundations of the building. There were some oarsmen who could show me around. All of a sudden I knew what it was like to be recruited—the feeling that an enormous and important institution wanted and was willing to look after me. I was ready to sign up.

I wondered what group I was to meet. My sister, Jennie, had filled me with stories of bitter feuds among the rowing squads. Her eight had made national news by protesting stark naked because the women had no showers at the boathouse. They had filed into the office of the director of women's athletics and disrobed as their captain read a statement about the rights of women guaranteed by Title IX. They got facilities soon afterward, but according to Jennie's description, the gym was seething with rebellion. The atmosphere I walked into, however, was light and easy.

Jennie is much more rebellious than I. For a woman to row, especially during those first years after Yale became coed, was a statement. Rowing exemplified the struggle of women to gain acceptance. They worked hard, were talented, and within a few years they won the national championships, but they were still targets of abuse. They had none of the Old Blue backing—and the men hated the contrast to their own miserable performance. The women's crew was particularly conscious of the traditions. They sang the songs and went through the motions more fervently than we ever did. But during those years they did not fit. Jennie had the drive and talent, but she was not tall or male. Although abashed by the lowly status of being an inexperienced freshman, I was already at home inside the door that Jennie struggled to open.

"A Few Minutes in the Fall"

In a college like Oxford or Cambridge, rowing does for those who practice it nearly everything that the rules of the authorities propose to do. It makes them lead a regular and simple life; it gets them out of bed early in the morning and sends them to bed again at ten at night; it disciplines them, it keeps them healthy, for it makes temperance necessary.... If I could only add that it forces a man to his books and necessarily made him a brilliant subject for examiners, I should have compiled a fairly complete list of academic virtues.

—R.C. LEHMAN,
The Complete Oarsman, 1909

When I was a freshman the simple demands of the sport carried me through the trauma of being new to

Yale. Rowing was a constructive form of play, a two-hour recess. At three o'clock every afternoon we put aside our books and jogged from the quiet seclusion of Yale through the surrounding decay of New Haven's inner residential district to the "lagoon," a thousand-meter reed-infested slough near the Yale Bowl.

Oblivious to the nature of boats, rowing and even the stench of the lagoon, we paddled about while Buzz followed in the launch. Until the basic rowing motions were established, little could be said to hurry the process. Buzz watched but was silent. We rowed two or four at a time while the others balanced the boat with their blades flat on the water. It would take several weeks for the boats to become reasonably stable with all eight rowing. In the meantime we dozed in our seats, careful only to maintain the set of the boat with the level of the oar handle. We rocked to the rhythm of the catch and the hiss of water under the oars—whispering, telling jokes, counting reeds along the bank. When my turn came I would splash about and then return to dozing.

We had more than thirty freshman heavyweights. Of our group, twelve had rowed in prep school. Most of the rest of us had never seen shells before. The best of the twelve experienced oarsmen were occasionally allowed to row with the varsity. Otherwise, their days must have been infinitely frustrating. Wallowing in eights after being stars at Exeter or St. Paul's. A thankless task. Experienced oarsmen sped the training of the novices, fighting frustration while the rest of us improved. The veterans must have realized that when the largest and most dedicated of us learned how to row, we would take their places.

Not until sophomore year, when I watched the next batch of freshmen, did I realize how poorly I had rowed.

In comparison, an unbalanced eggbeater would have seemed graceful. From the stroke seat, Biglow could feel us rush up the slides, slam into the slide stops, hesitate, and then drop our blades into the water. I didn't know Biglow then, and I suppose I did not want to know him until I had a chance of keeping up with him. In the meantime, I kept in the company of the other inexperienced oarsmen and stayed oblivious to the misery we caused those who already knew how to row. For me rowing fulfilled a dream. It furnished a sense of purpose, a continuity from day to day. My best friends in high school had also come east to school and were dreadfully homesick. I too was homesick, but I could look toward the spring as the racing season rather than as just another series of courses.

My elder brother was graduated Phi Beta Kappa from Swarthmore College and then went to Athens to study archaeology. My sister was graduated magna cum laude, carrying six courses and rowing at the same time. When my first paper was returned, the first of six 6-page essays for introductory psychology, I flung the C− across my bedroom and left for practice. Alumni and athletic preference, I reminded myself.

In the fall there should have been time for both practice and study. Rowing began as only a small time commitment each day, and as the time increased, we learned to cope—or so went the theory. I still laugh each year when I see the freshman recruiting propaganda that is distributed each fall. Nowadays, the coaches don't have to stretch the truth to make the program sound successful, but they still advertise that freshman practice time is limited to sixty minutes a day in the beginning and will not increase beyond ninety minutes in the fall.

It might have been sixty minutes the first week and ninety for the next three, but after a month the time commitment increased exponentially. For the most part we were all eager to have more time to row, although we never knew what we were getting ourselves into. In the meantime, our lives were wild, frenetic—so many new experiences and so few hours.

At 9:10 one morning I had stumbled into my nine o'clock class. Sometimes when I was late I ran the last bit to look tired, as if I really tried to be on time. This time I didn't have to.

I suppose I should have gone back to bed. I had finished the paper at midnight and had been in bed by two, but inexplicably the phone had rung at five minutes to six. My roommate, bless his soul, took the call and was more than a little angry when told that the bus was waiting to take me to practice.

Not only was I late, but the practice was late and consequently most of us were late to class. Unshowered, unshaven, almost delirious with fatigue, I had run to class to turn in the paper. Ten minutes late, I stood in the open doorway of the lecture hall.

Mason Lab room 211 was a modern lecture hall by Yale standards. A white Formica laboratory table was at the focus of the small amphitheater. Radiating from the focus were rows of white tables rising stepwise into the distance. Chromium seats swiveled from under each table. I have been told the room looks like the United Nations General Assembly. As I looked up from the podium, the concrete, chrome and harsh white lights seemed more reminiscent of a KGB interrogation chamber. My entrance was behind and to the left of the podium. The hall was filled to capacity. The professor

105

stopped lecturing and indicated an empty seat in the front row. Vacantly I walked over and slouched into the chrome.

Someone was tapping my shoulder. It couldn't be time for practice. I looked up blankly, focusing finally into the professor's eyes. They shouldn't be this close, I thought. Then it dawned on me that we were alone, and the clock said that it was 10:05. The class had been over for ten minutes and my notebook had less than two lines written since the beginning of class. "You can go now" was all he said.

Had I concluded then that rowing would seriously detract from academics, I doubt that I could have quit. I was obsessed with the desire to do something well, to achieve distinction. I needed an identity to stand against the unquestioned excellence of those around me. In psychology class I read Fels's study arguing that boys who do well in athletics are nonacademically inclined while those who are incompetent in athletics avoid them and pursue academics. The choice between athletics and academics is made during preadolescence according to which of the two maximizes the likelihood of success and decreases the possibility of failure. Few do both athletics and academics successfully. Upon reading Freud, I had developed neuroses. Reading Fels, I concluded that while I had once been able to vacillate between athletics and scholarship, a choice would now have to be made. The A on my second paper postponed the decision.

Most of us would have been categorized as having initially chosen academics: potentially good athletes but not jocks. We would walk back from practice each evening wondering why we engaged in such an odd and painful activity. In my one year of high school football, the fundamental question "Why play?" never arose. At some time well before I joined the football team, the players had become athletes. Devoutly religious people don't have to understand the essence of their faith. So too if one grows up with his father passing him footballs. Who needs an excuse for playing when no one asks why?

To my knowledge, my father never had the slightest interest in sports. He had also played football in high school but only because the team would have had too few players without him. My elder brother and sister read books the way most children watch television. I also missed the early indoctrinations of elementary school. Two days too young to enter public school, I went to an alternative private school. I learned to climb trees, build forts, do math problems and eventually to read; but there were no sports. There were no fields for ball games and no pavement for basketball; in fact, competition itself was discouraged. After three weeks at the school I was kicked up to the next grade—not because I was smart but because I was big. I had exerted "negative leadership," encouraging others to climb trees from which they could not get down.

When transferred to public school in the second grade, I had yet to learn the fundamentals of sports. I found my recess niche as the champion tetherball player, a two-man game with a ball connected by a rope to the top of a pole. The object of the game is to hit the ball over the head of your opponent so that it wraps the rope tightly around the pole. Being tall made it easy.

Being tall made a lot of things easy. While harmless and inept at fighting, I was seldom challenged. On fitness tests I was always near the top of my class but did nothing with it. Great potential, I was always told, so I got good at quitting—at being cajoled into trying out

107

for a sport and then deciding that I really had better things to do.

I played football my senior year in high school largely because the coaches had stopped asking me to. Then I had to prove that I could. A special glory was reserved for the football team, the kind of glory that epitomized the conflict between jocks and academics. Considering the amount of time and dedication necessary to make the team, I suppose football players deserved more glory than, for example, the student body president; but the time and dedication were not ostensibly what shaped the team.

I worked harder to make the football team than for anything I had tried before, but even when I succeeded, I was not satisfied. As a game it was a lot of fun, but like rowing, football was a way of life. The instinctual immediacy which makes the game so exciting renders it and its players intellectually careless. Fury takes over from precision. I learned that I could generally have my way by being big, and if being that didn't work by itself, being big and angry would. After a while, I believed that we deserved the glory, that the band, the crowd and the cheerleaders were all just for us.

At Yale the differences between oarsmen and football players led to some problems. Both teams were large and aggressive, but had different methods of venting aggression. During the fall, the football team and the crew got back to campus at the same time. At about seven o'clock one hundred hungry football players and oarsmen descended upon the Freshman Commons. The Commons was a great, cavernous building on the scale of an urban train station, but despite its size a fifteen-minute wait in line was standard. All was quiet, however, so long as the football team's bus got back to Commons first. They would then charge to the front of the line, arguing (if anyone happened to ask) that they were late to dinner because they had no choice. Anyone else could have come to dinner earlier. Until the crew beat the football team back from practice, there were no problems.

After one bitterly cold practice in late October, we hurried back to eat. We arrived at Commons before seven and, more importantly, before the football team. Fifty or so of us were standing patiently, playing anagrams with the letters on the menu board, when the freshman football team arrived. While deciding what to do with the extra *P* after changing "BOILED POTATOES AND SHRIMP CREOLE" into "MASHED CRETIN TOE BOILS" and "APE DROOL," I was hit from behind. I turned, half expecting an enraged cretin or a drooling ape, but met, instead, a lineman.

They did have a good system. They rounded the corner by the ticket lady slowly enough to check off their names and then accelerated toward the line. At the time of collision, they would be traveling fast enough that people stepped aside.

Two or three battered through before Eric and I attempted to hold our position. We stood side by side facing back toward the football team. I didn't even have time to say "Red Rover" before the first struck. He slammed between us and was almost through before we stopped his forward progress.

"First and ten?"

"What the hell? I'm on the football team!" he explained.

We did not let go. The rest of his team, confronted by this knot in the line, could not get by either. They informed us that their coach allowed them to cut in line.

Meanwhile, the one we held was growing hostile. I considered removing my glasses but doing so would have seemed provocative and too melodramatic.

In different sports there are different types of pain. In football pain is divided into short increments. As one leaves the line, there is a momentary acceleration and then impact. Commitment and then crunch. Football players soon learn that objects with greater mass and velocity sustain less damage.

I considered the nature of the impact as I imagined that lineman's fist crunching my glasses. The pains of rowing might be more intense than such an impact, but the pain of rowing is controlled, nurtured. One cannot simply abandon himself to the consequence of momentum. I was not very good at just abandoning myself to consequences.

The previous summer during an altercation with a couple of muggers, I dodged one assailant's baseball bat, turned and impacted with the fist of his confederate. I learned then that it is possible to absorb a punch in the jaw and shake it off, but it is not an experience worth repeating; luckily, a couple of the other football players took hold of their mate, and we all spent an amiable few minutes in line.

The goal of athletics is control over the body—discipline and the testing of limits. Unleashing one's body without discipline is against the spirit of sport. My senior year, another member of the football team heard that I was writing about sports and demanded quite forcefully that I explain the philosophy of football. I answered that I did not believe there is a philosophy of football—nor is there a philosophy of baseball, crew or running. The relationship between the mind and body, the quest for excellence: these are the philosophically interesting topics. To lose control over the body and its emotions is to lose philosophic and, I believe, athletic value.

The danger of becoming an athlete is the tendency to see problems as physical obstacles. Sophomore year, I remember commanding a teaching assistant to remedy an injustice. He had given me no credit on an important lab report because I had turned in the carbon copy of my data rather than the original. When I had handed him my report, he had not complained about the copy, but even when I brought him the original from my notebook, he refused to grade it. He said it was too late. Before I became a successful athlete and so conscious of my body, I would have gone to the professor in charge and asked for arbitration, but I was beyond reason. This teaching assistant seemed to derive such pleasure from the power he held. The lab was completely quiet, listening. "Don't worry, he's not pre-med," my lab partner whispered rather too loudly across the room.

"You don't understand," I said finally. "I am not asking you to grade this. I am telling you, and you are going to do it right now!" My voice trembled with rage. My hands were clenched. I had no idea what to do next, but it must have looked like I was going to dismember him. He did what he was told, but had the last laugh giving out grades at the end of the term. At the time, however, it was worth it.

For me during that first year of rowing, the emergence of an athlete was becoming increasingly arduous. Every week practice ended a little later and extra workouts became more frequent. The five-mile runs every Saturday morning soon became a warm-up for the work-

out in the gym. Those Saturday practices were a nui-
sance in themselves; more importantly, they meant that
Friday night had to be cut short. All the while the squad
was shrinking. I didn't remember many names, but familiar faces were absent. Soon we were down from four
to three eights. We had more time to practice because
there was no need for two practice sessions. We were
also rowing better and beginning to work hard in the
shells. As time went on, the cumulative effects of a
smaller squad, better oarsmen and more time on the
water made practice much more substantial. Rather than
return from practice invigorated, I would moan in time
to the stereo.

By mid-October the thousand meters of the lagoon
became too short, so we joined the varsity on the yellow
school bus to the Housatonic River at Derby, Connecticut, a twenty-five-minute ride out beyond the lagoon
and the Yale Bowl that I was to catch promptly at 3:45
every fall and spring weekday for the next four years.
The two hours jumped to about three and a half hours
with the bus ride and longer practices.

From the road alongside the Housatonic River, the
Yale boathouse appears graceful but unprepossessing.
The pueblolike stack of rectangular white stucco boxes
is traced in blue and topped with Spanish clay shingles:
quaint but plain in comparison to the ornamentation of
the Harvard and Penn boathouses.

The inside too is plain. Aside from the plaque com-
memorating the building of the boathouse, very little
gives any indication of the traditions—nothing like the
timelessness of the Ferry—just white plaster, bare locker
rooms, tiled showers and a few old oars hanging about.
Tony had talked of decorating the place for years, but
I don't believe the trappings were really important to

him. He once lost track of his Olympic silver medal for more than a year!

Down two flights of wooden steps are the four boat bays. Freshman year, there were three bays until the women stripped and the fourth was built—not tradition but constant evolution. Freshman year, the majority of the boats were wooden. Four years later, wooden shells were scarce among boats made of fiber glass or carbon fiber.

On my first trips to Derby, I was overwhelmed. The size of the boathouse, the enormous number of shells and the electric aura left me completely uncritical: a typical, wide-eyed freesh, as we were called by the varsity. Not for quite some time did I even wonder why our boathouse was not cluttered with trophies and regatta banners like Harvard's and Penn's. The varsity had that cocky, self-righteous air about them that was everything I expected from the best crew in the country. I imagined that they no longer bothered with the paraphernalia of success. They were godlike, and, quite frankly, I did not want to associate with them until I was good enough to compete. Perhaps that is why it was the middle of the spring before I understood why there were no trophies. The varsity didn't win! They were better my freshman year than Yale had been in many years and they were mediocre. My heroes, to whom I would make such an effort not to pay homage to because I believed they were so much better than I, were preserving a fabrication. To hear them talk, they were undefeated.

During my senior year there were still no trophies at the boathouse. We had won quite a few but we never got around to hanging them. Leaving things at the boathouse didn't seem to matter then, but I wonder. The trophies and photographs at Harvard give the boathouse an aura of success. Even their freshmen seem to believe that the trophies are theirs. They may row better for them.

I pushed on, unaware that what I was committing my college career to had been a failure and almost a joke for more than a decade; fortunately, my misconceptions lasted until I had invested so much that the truth did not change my own expectations. With twenty-four oarsmen looking for seats in the first freshman eight, there was no time to worry about the varsity; meanwhile, our freshman crew was becoming more of a unit. In the rush to find new friends, we went out of our way to be friendly to one another, knowing all the while that we would soon be fighting for the same places. We pushed one another for the sake of the group and then each did a little extra to stay ahead of the pack.

It was an easy relationship. Eager to explore the new combinations of muscles, those of us new to rowing attacked the workouts with a blissful naïveté. We threw ourselves into the pieces heedless of the terrible set of the boats. The experienced oarsmen tried to tell us that there was more to it than exertion, but it was like teaching music to the tone-deaf. Rowing seemed so marvelously physical.

On through October and November we practiced out at Derby. We did have a brief race in Cambridge the morning of the Harvard football game, but even that small victory mattered little. Real racing would not begin until April. By then we would have trained seven months for that first six-minute ordeal. Twenty-four hours of practice for each minute of race. I enjoyed the work except when Buzz would become exasperated with my technique. Driving the launch just outside the reach of the oars, he called to me at every catch. "Late...

late...late...good...late...good...." For miles on end he would call at each stroke. I felt no difference between being a blade behind everyone else and being "on time." The boat seemed to go the same speed whether I was late or not, but Buzz kept yelling and I kept imagining all sorts of different ways to get through the same motion. Eventually, it became a matter of perverse pride to find how terribly I could row and still, by working hard, make the team. A football player's approach to rowing.

As days got shorter, time on the water became more precious. Buzz often tried unsuccessfully to squeeze in extra pieces before dark. We finished with our blades flashing in the glare of Buzz's spotlight. At least in the dark the spotlight would tell whom Buzz was watching.

Like blind men we developed our other senses. If being blind helped, I wondered about being deaf, dumb, insensitive and boring. Couldn't hurt, I supposed. As was once said of the riverboat captain who guided his boat through the most treacherous stretch of the Mississippi while sleepwalking, "If he can do that while he is asleep, imagine what he could do if he were dead!"

The Derby Bank electronic sign marked our progress into December. Four o'clock, it read as we drove past on the bus. Four o'clock, sixty degrees, fifty, thirty-four, twenty-two. So as not to get our socks wet before practice, we carried the boat barefoot over the ice-covered dock. Then we would warm up in the shell, overheating under layers of sweat clothes while unable to bend our frozen hands from the oar. Being from California, I found it disconcerting to spit on the oar and have to shatter the frozen spittle, but Buzz believed in maximizing "water time." The more time we were able to row in the fall, the faster we would be in the spring.

It was new, different and invigorating. When people asked why I did it or were awed by our abuses in the snow, we just smiled. How much better to be deemed crazy by people I respected than to be deemed narrow-minded.

Committed

The Sunday morning following that first Christmas vacation, John and I returned to Derby. Gusts of wind swirled the dusty snow like tumbleweeds across a Death Valley ghost town. Inside was the same. White and barren. Downstairs the boats hung gloomily in the racks, forgotten until spring. A fresh spray of snow followed the familiar rumble of the opening bay doors, but still nothing awoke. Our river, our racecourse, was asleep. The old, half-submerged wooden launches were locked in ice. I grabbed John's arm and pulled him outside, skating the icy ramp to the dock and beyond onto the frozen flow. Together we set off across the racecourse, imagining the lane markers, calling strokes, yelling ratings. We walked faster, the cadence increasing. "I've got six seats and I want more," I yelled, pulling ahead.

Biglow broke into a run, regaining the lead across the ice. I went with him, matching him stride for stride. Our feet threw up the snow, leaving swirling clouds behind. As we approached the finish, John began to sprint. Knowing that I could not beat him, I lunged, grappled with his feet and took him down. Bad luck to catch a crab with less than ten meters to go. John was miffed, but Fate could not have intended that we end our first race on foot. We dusted off the snow and returned to campus for the first practice of the new year.

According to the great American boatbuilder and rowing sage Stan Pocock, the three R's of rowing are "Rowing, Rowing and Rowing." Pocock, however, is from Seattle. Oarsmen on the East Coast can find substitute winter exercises for conditioning, but no substitute will improve rowing technique. Mechanical rowing machines of the type that I will describe later can fill some of the technical gaps, but no machine adequately simulates the feel of a boat. The ideal solution (other than flying south) is to create a river indoors.

Rivers travel well but don't take to captivity. When confined, they assume other identities—lakes, puddles, Perrier—but not all of these are useful to the oarsman. One may ask what is wrong with the stagnant form of the species. For example, why not fix an eight into the swimming pool? It is done but there are good reasons not to. First of all, the rhythmic splashing of the oars upsets the swim team. Secondly, an indoor shell is, of course, stationary. Pulling a full-size spoon-bladed oar through stagnant water from a stationary shell is arduous work—good for initial technique, brute strength and elongated arms. Another option is to decrease the size of the blade or use "hollow" blades, oars that have the center of the blades cut out. Decreasing the surface of the blade makes higher cadences possible but still does not approximate a true catch or release in moving water. To row in a stationary shell, one must capture the spirit as well the corpus of the river.

The main basement of the Payne Whitney Gymnasium is divided into three rooms the size of small airplane hangars: one room each for the heavyweight, lightweight and women's crews. Caged inside a concrete tank along the wall of each room is a small river. The tank platform is enormous, nearly 70 feet long, 20 feet wide and about 3 feet high. Not only does each river fit precisely into its own tank but it consents to be divided by the concrete shell that runs lengthwise through its middle. The shells are fitted with slides and footstretchers like regular eights. While there are no outriggers, each shell is the width of one of the old racing barges. Oarlocks are mounted along the edges.

Most of the time, the casual observer would conclude that there are three very dead lakes. They do lie motionless, often for months on end, but then they are napping. Now the difference between a napping river and a dead lake is the dynamic potential. If one were to feed fifteen-dollars-an-hour worth of electricity into an ordinary dead lake, one would discover a lot of dead fish. Not so with Yale's sleeping rivers.

The secret is to capture a continuous loop of river— to take a long straight stretch and connect the ends like a hoop snake biting its tail. Although the river is naturally lazy, if one then zaps it with enough electricity, it wakes up and circulates like a conveyor belt.

Encouraging the river's circulation via oars was our major training during the winter. The concrete shell gave a stable base from which to improve technique while approximating a moving shell, encouraging novices to pull hard without fear of upsetting the boat. The major difference is that one rowed on a solid platform.

When the people at MIT built their new boathouse a few years ago, they tried to simulate a floating shell. With rollers, springs and pulleys they essentially suspended a shell above their captive river so that oarsmen would have to maintain the set. The boat was also designed to accelerate against powerful springs, simulating the longitudinal as well as lateral forces in rowing. It didn't work. Why? I don't know. Whatever the mistake, within days of its christening, they welded all the moving parts together.

In any tank, the scenery doesn't change much no matter how long one rows. Mirrors line the side rails to help with technical problems but even the most narcissistic grows tired of watching himself. Furthermore, the only way to keep the timing correct is to watch the man in front. In a real shell one can unconsciously follow the rhythm, freeing the mind to limitless speculation. In tanks, such speculation precedes the impact of the following oar handle into one's kidneys.

Even the river quickly becomes bored with the surroundings, venting its frustration into the heated basement air. Within minutes, progeny of our tamed river condensed in insidious places. Sometimes I contemplated the rivulets that formed along my arms. Back and forth they ebbed, the volume and distance increasing with each passing minute. Eventually, breakers crashed over the wrist onto my hands. The oar handle first became slippery and then gritty, the worn skin wearing away at what was left. No, I was not fond of the tanks, but they did provide relief from weight circuits and stairs.

I mentioned that the Payne Whitney Gymnasium is fourteen stories high. That is not officially true. When the gym was built, a civil code prohibited buildings with more than nine stories, but the code did not take into account mezzanines. Hence, after the fifth floor is 5B, 6, 6B, all the way to 9B. To get to the top there are three perfectly functional elevators, several small fire staircases and a luxuriously wide main stairway—wide enough for four large oarsmen to ascend abreast. The steps look similar to the stone entry steps to the law school, both stairways worn with the tread of the ages. Both buildings were built in the thirties. At the law school, the tread of the ages was etched within thirty minutes by a powerful sandblaster. "Antiquing," they call it. At the gym, the process is simply called "stairs." It takes longer to achieve the same effect, but it's more organic.

The procedure was to run the 187 steps from 5 to 9B, hurry down and repeat the exercise up to ten times. Unlike most of our long-interval rowing in the tanks, the stairs were anaerobic exercise—minute-long bursts that consumed oxygen at a much higher rate than it could be replaced. The initial result was an oxygen-deficient high. The stone walls wavered and melted, comfortably constricting, as one rounded the bend for the next flight. Up and up the tunnel continued, echoing with the steps and gasps of those preceding. I just followed the handrail, never looking up until 7B, and then checking every floor thereafter. The light was broken at 7B. Had I ever looked up at 7 or 6B, I would probably have stopped before the top.

Harvard doesn't do stairs. They do "stadiums." Despite the pretentious title, it is the same sort of preparation for those last five hundred meters, where everything is gone but the boat continues.

The most insidious training is derived from the most innocuous source. Weight circuits, as they are called, are just a series of exercises with a relatively light barbell. The procedure is simple. One grasps the bar, repeats an exercise ten times, and then without dropping the bar continues with ten repetitions of the next exercise. Altogether, there are seven exercises which are repeated without rest. It's straightforward the first time through and maybe the first three or four, but each set takes two minutes and we repeated sets for thirty. When the *Mercury* astronauts were chosen, the largest part of the training was to desensitize them. The instantaneous reactions of the test pilots chosen for the program were not useful in the fully automated *Mercury* capsule. The astronauts had to be trained not to touch anything, to endure. I sometimes think that is what we were trained to do—to endure so much that races became easy by comparison.

For two months after Christmas vacation we limped around campus with muscles too tight and sore to walk properly, yet we had no good idea of our goal. Without knowing what a real race was like, I couldn't judge whether it was worth all the preparation, but having put in so much time already, how could we back out? Quite a few freshmen did manage to back out. After Christmas several, when freed from daily practice, decided that they liked not feeling tired all the time. Most of them vanished without a word.

The first to quit were those who could not take the work. The next were the solid intellectual types out for the quick-fix transcendental experience, the oneness of body, mind, machine and river that sounds good in conversation. Those people, who knew what they wanted, realized that it wasn't worth the price. They had carefully balanced the options and saw that the balance was not to be had rowing. That is what I suppose happened; none of them was ever good at explaining for himself.

Those of us who stayed were younger, more tractable. Less sure of ourselves socially and intellectually, we gave ourselves to the sport with little idea of what we could give or receive. Sports appeal initially to the younger, more basic emotions: aggression, physical toughness. Outsiders think that rowing produces fanatics, but I think that potential fanaticism is just more recognizable when given a focus like rowing.

Years later I watched as a friend's little brother was hooked by lightweight rowing. He had never been athletic, but he found rowing a challenge. He was a determined sort, a perfectionist, and rowing appeared such a definite and easily attainable perfection. What novice would believe that it takes years to master the technique? In the meantime, to give up would be to admit defeat. I once almost admired those who could break away. I thought that they were strong enough to look an addiction in the face and say no. Now I am too much of a believer. I might still try to warn his brother (or mine) about what he was getting into, but I doubt he would listen. I wouldn't have listened. The warning would have been like a glove in the face. The only fate worse would be not to try.

For me there had been no time of crisis; instead, the crew became more of a home as time went by. That year it seemed that everything that could have been questioned, broken or belittled was. Each new void that Yale created was filled again by the crew. My worry was not whether to keep rowing but whether I would earn a seat in the first freshman boat.

At that time I was still true to my girl friend from high school, who had gone on to Stanford. We clung together by long-distance telephone, convincing each other that we were worth waiting for, but by February we were distant. She asked me if I planned to return to California during my spring vacation, but I didn't hesitate before saying no. The crew would be training in Florida for those two weeks.

I remember her phone call the night of the crew banquet at Mory's, asking if I would mind if she went out with some Stanford senior. We could try again that summer, she said. Did I mind? California seemed so far away. I tried appealing to what I thought would be the latent Penelope in all women. Wouldn't you rather just stay home and weave until I finish racing? I suppose in the good old days I would have then flown home and put an arrow through his gizzard, but making the team seemed much more important. As it was, I went to Mory's for the second hard-line American defense.

The old drinking song was getting slower, each syllable being dragged interminably. "For I'm H A P P Y to be F R double E." The letters each reverberated through the oaken rooms. "F R double E from the bonds of S I N." The syrupy red potion of grenadine and rum flowed down my throat. The gallon-sized silver goblet slowly emptied, the song dragged on. I could not pass the cup until they finished my song and they were barely halfway. Dave Potter tucked a napkin into my collar like a bib as the red goo ran down my chin.

As I drank beneath their photograph, the "Gutless Crew" of '22 smiled down. After a poor early season the crew of '22 had been labeled "gutless" by their own coach in a letter that made its way into *The New York Times*. With their coxswain chanting "Gutless" at each catch, the same crew had then passed Harvard in the final strokes of the Race. The photograph was taken as the coxswain stepped over the unconscious stroke to shake hands with the seven man.

"Sing hallelujah!" The red cup was almost gone, the white napkin was being spread on the table. "Sing hallelujah!" Vertical, upside down, it revolved over my lips, draining the last drops from the rim. "Put a nickel on the drum and you'll be saved!"

Rim first, the silver goblet crashed onto the white napkin.

"One!" Did I make it?

"Two!" A red spot on the napkin and I would lose.

"Three!" I hoisted the cup by its massive silver handles.

"Clean!" It wasn't the Race but I did pass out in the arms of my comrades. I lost my girl friend, I missed the next morning's midterm exam, but I had survived my first eastern winter and made the squad for the two-week spring training in Florida. For the moment that was enough.

By March, after six months of training, that first racing season was less than a month away. Buzz had four weeks on the water before our first race in which to improve our technique enough to row over 30 strokes per minute and select the first eight. What he also would do during that month was convince us of our own mania. Previously there had been grueling tests of our determination, but the work had increased so gradually that it generally seemed reasonable. Florida gave a chance for the unreasonable.

Five o'clock one Friday afternoon in early March three chartered buses, filled to capacity with the Yale rowing squads, set off for Tampa. I folded myself into a seat beside another freshman who was 6 feet 7 and soon we were leaving the freezing rain of New Haven for the twenty-four-hour journey, each of us armed with all sorts of semi-edibles from the dining hall. If I had been smart I would have arranged to sit next to one of the coxswains, but I counted on being able to stretch out at the rest stops. I had not known that during those twenty-four hours we would stop only once—for fifteen minutes.

My choice of seat had not been completely my own fault. I put my belongings in a seat about five rows back from the front and had then left for a few moments. When I returned, my luggage was in the aisle, and a senior was in my seat. "A Senior Rules Committee expropriation," he explained airily. I had never heard of the SRC, but it seemed no time to argue, so I moved back.

During that ride I still imagined that the varsity were rowing gods, so when they made life difficult for others I excused them. My sister was rowing on the women's crew, who were then as now national champions, yet I said nothing when the upperclassmen referred to them as "cracks." Not until I was a sophomore did I try to stop them. I did not understand why the varsity then put so much effort into making life unpleasant for the women, lightweights and even the freshmen when we were all dedicated to the same task; but being in the varsity boat was my dream, so it was hard not to emulate them. The SRC, I found out later, was never more than an amusing game until after 1963, the last year we beat Harvard. The worse the crew became, the more vocal the SRC. The SRC found fault with everyone else's accomplishments to excuse the varsity's failure. The only oarsmen I knew who stood up to the SRC when I was a freshman were Ted, Joe and Andy—the sophomores with whom I would win two Eastern Championships.

Several of the upperclassmen my freshman year had disliked Ted, Joe, Andy, just as they came to dislike me and many of my class because they thought we were, of all things, "cocky." Of course we were cocky! We were the new generation of Yale oarsmen. We had been led to believe that the Yale crew was great and when we discovered the deception, we set about making a change. Our predecessors considered fellowship and longevity on the team more important than winning races. I believed that fellowship would improve when we won the races. The next year in Florida, the captain of the crew and I battled for the same seat. We were the same size and roughly the same strength, but he was a senior and I a sophomore. We would both probably have been in the varsity; however, before the selection was made, he developed a hernia. I remember shaking his hand in the dining hall at Tampa before he flew home for the operation, knowing that we were losing a fine oarsmen, but not at all worried about the effect of his absence on the boat. The seniors had lost for too long. They were not cocky.

Twenty-three hours and one fifteen-minute break later, we arrived in Tampa. I had gotten a few hours' sleep in the luggage rack and a few minutes in a hammock slung in the aisle, but still I had been cramped far too long. I was not prepared for the fantastical and absurd apparition that was the University of Tampa, our home for the next two weeks.

The main building of the university was covered with onions, not real onions but towers that approximated onions while attempting a Disney imitation of minarets. The "mosque" supporting these onions was built as a hotel during the nineties, which went broke and eventually became the university.

The school once had a football team that had advanced a few players to the pros, but the team became

127

too expensive. When the team died, so did the school. They now had no focus, no goals, no academic traditions and no football team. They did have a crew, but in the preceding year nine of their oarsmen were dropped for failing to maintain a 2.0 grade point average. Most of the students spent their days by the pool, like the octogenarians at the nearby retirement community. The sun beat down, the hair lightened, the skin darkened, the brain frazzled, and the boredom increased.

The first dinner we tried to impress the locals. We donned regulation Ivy League coat and tie, put napkins in our laps, tried not to fart, and ate with moderation. Monday morning they saw our true selves at breakfast: dripping in the crowded, narrow corridor, wearing briny, sweat-soaked rowing gear, while stealing all the doughnuts and making the regular students late for class. Within a few days at least one Tampette wrote a scathing letter to *The Minaret,* the house organ, about our personal habits; but the paper was a weekly effort, so by the time the student body mobilized resistance, we were gone.

After a week in Tampa, though, we were no longer the lusty, swaggering giants who had arrived to conquer. I think we were all uncertain and cowed. Although I had survived double practices in football, I felt unprepared. On top of the building fatigue was the knowledge that the first boat would soon be selected. In retrospect I realize that with one or two exceptions that freshman boat had chosen itself. From the beginning there were the obvious candidates from the experienced group. like Biglow, Jim Millar and Dave Potter. Then there were the second group of inexperienced but large and fit oarsmen, like me and Eric. As time wore on, the top group sought each other out, instinctively preferring one another's company to those who were not doing so well. Eric and I commiserated with each other as we walked back from the dining hall because we were both convinced that the other would have nothing to worry about but that our own position was precarious. Commiserating with those who were destined for the second or third boats was much more difficult. It detracted from the happiness of one's own success.

Through that first week we all made a point to appear eager. Fortunately, only one practice a day had been scheduled for the weekend. One practice was not a vacation, but Buzz told us that we would be able to sleep late that Saturday and have an easy row at ten o'clock. With the prospect of sleeping late before an easy workout, most of us went out Friday night to ease the tension.

By ten o'clock in the morning Tampa approached ninety degrees. Already sweating, we hoisted the boats from the shade of the willows out to the brackish water of the Hillsborough River. Both because it was to be only a short practice, and because we had previously rowed only at dawn and early evening, most of us neglected hats and suntan lotion. Many had their shirts off. As justification for spending the two-week vacation rowing, we all felt obligated to be tanned by the time we returned to New Haven. Still, I felt no joy in the brilliance of the sunshine. I thought only of the strength leached and the hours wasted in worship of the Tampa sun god.

That day, instead of heading downstream toward Tampa Bay, we followed the Hillsborough upstream. Stroke after stroke we twisted up the narrow, sweaty canal at three-quarter pressure, repeating monotonous pieces as the temperature climbed and the humidity approached rain. Skin boiled in sweat that could not evaporate. The salt crusted our shorts, festering the sores, but it was to be a light workout, so we would turn back soon. Between pieces we would look to Buzz for the inevitable command to turn the boats around. Anticipation of that command made each stroke more painful, fading our inquiring glances into vacant glassiness. Betrayed, beyond all landmarks, we continued.

Eight miles up, we ran out of river. An empty stream, a great silence. Dispirited, parched, choking down the cottony air, we prepared to turn back. My eyes followed Buzz, wondering if he felt the hatred. Gripped in one hand was his megaphone; in the other, a quart of water. I would have drooled like one of Pavlov's dogs upon seeing the bottle, but the salt crust on my lips was impenetrable. I just watched as Buzz ordered the boats to turn around and took a swig from the bottle, a short draft like he really didn't need it. Next he would pour the remainder into the river, I imagined. My eyes trailed the bottle out over the side. Good God! He was going to pour the water over the side. I marveled at the power, the single-minded strength of purpose, capable of such horror. A power unbounded, such as I had never encountered before. Fascinating, compelling, while we moaned in complete, deathlike indifference. Purposefully, Buzz's arm swung back, cocked and tossed the bottle out over the river—into the waiting hands of the other boat's coxswain. August benevolence. A power for good unbounded. Eighteen people and a quart of water. I followed the bottle from lip to lip down the boats, took my sip and followed it again. I remember pausing before the drink, wondering if this were not the sort of communion I should refuse, but being eight miles from rest, he owned our souls. No current in this river could bring us back. I drank and wondered only what he would command.

"Full pressure to the boathouse, build to full in three!"

I don't think anyone even managed a complaint. Despondently but without questions, the boats began to move. Who would commit himself to full pressure for eight miles? But hesitation served only to throw off the set of the boat. The brackish spray stung the opening sores on our hands. The river twisted and turned, the three bridges I remembered on the way up turned into six. With each bridge I imagined that we were close and resolved to pull harder, only to be greeted five or ten minutes later by yet another. After four bridges I began to mumble. "I quit" accented each release. The shirt wadded at my feet shaded only the bottom of the shell. My cap lay in the boathouse. With the sun pounding my bare head I left the shell for the Foreign Legion. Beau Geste, legionnaire, buried to his neck in sand and left to die. As Buzz became the maniacal sergeant, I began to laugh. Shrill, empty laughter. Eric, in front of me, was crying.

On the dock Eric said he was quitting. He sounded so apologetic, as if he had failed us. The strongest, most dutiful man in the boat believed he had failed us. He went to inform Buzz, but Eric could not quit. He would never let us down. Anyway, it was too late. The worst was over.

That morning each of us found a breaking point. Not only a physical barrier, but a point where determination, stamina and duty clashed and were overcome not so much by pain but by absurdity.

As Thorstein Veblen writes in *The Theory of the Leisure Class:*

purposeless physical exertion is tedious and distasteful beyond tolerance....Recourse in such cases has to be some form of activity which shall at least afford a colorable pretence of purpose, even if the object assigned be only a make-believe. Sports satisfy these requirements of substantial futility together with a colorable make-believe of purpose.

That row, we pulled through any make-believe of purpose, beyond all pretense, to where the task had no purpose. We reached that point yet kept working. For me fantasy filled the void. Eric's mind stayed in the boat. There the only reasonable decision was to quit.

Miraculously, Sunday's practice became a trip to Disney World. Like children we followed Buzz to safety amid singing Tiki birds and dancing bears, a happy family once again. We had endured, and from that point onward we could not quit. My vision of Hell is to row at full pressure in a boat without swing in the Florida sunshine.

The First Wake

When we were learning the craft of rowing, we belonged to Buzz. He was the artist molding us to his form. In Florida, I once rode in the launch for part of one practice while Buzz was choosing the first boat. I sat in the bow while he drove the launch, calculated stroke cadences, switched oarsmen between the two eights, and wrote notes about each of us: all the while laughing and cursing to himself. We were his creation. On the water we came to see ourselves through his eyes, molded as we were in his image. Once we had achieved the basic form, however, we were no longer just reflections of his art. Individuals reemerged to form the character of the boat. What characterized our freshman boat was the realization of the big lie.

As freshmen we bowed before the varsity for the six months preceding the races. Even when I had suspected that they were not working as hard as we freshmen I still bowed, imagining that their superior technical skills replaced brute force. As the year wore on, however, I began to realize the truth.

The Tuesday practice following the Northeastern race, my freshman boat was to do practice pieces with the varsity. We had never beaten them, but even early in the season we had come close. Each time we got closer, my distaste for their arrogance increased. The day was approaching when we would win.

The previous Saturday, I had felt physically ill when the varsity trailed Northeastern across the finish line. Northeastern was mediocre yet Yale lost. Humiliated beside the cheering Northeastern fans, I stalked off to reconsider the arrogance of my old heroes. I wanted to be like the varsity, to share in their tradition of triumph, but the still-damp Northeastern racing shirt slung at my own waist declared that we freshmen were different. The seniors might not place the premium on performance, but we would. That Tuesday we rowed out in a multicolored array of sweat shirts to meet the varsity, pulled even and prepared to race.

"Are you ready!...Ready all!" Either Buzz or Tony called the commands.

"Wait a second!" our coxswain chimed in.

"Oh, boys..." we yodeled across to the varsity boat, as in one motion we peeled off our sweats, exposing our full complement of white-and-red striped tank tops with "NORTHEASTERN" across the chest. We must have been a grand sight in the spring sun. The varsity didn't think us so grand, but then we were always willing to prove ourselves on the water.

A few days before the Harvard race that year, one of the varsity shaved his head. I could have accepted the gesture if they had a chance of winning, but it seemed more pretense. Harvard didn't need to shave their heads. Maybe having a shaved head made him pull harder—a victor looking like an idiot is more attractive than a loser in the same condition—but when they lost, I wanted to wrap my Harvard freshman shirt around his throat for making us all look like idiots.

Twenty freshmen were then on the squad: the first eight, second eight, and third four. Of those twenty, seventeen rowed the next year, and three years later seven of that first eight were still competing. We put so much emphasis on proving ourselves in competition, of not talking big if we could not match it with speed, that it became impossible for us to stop. Our mania cost a few casualties from our own ranks, those who were not capable of making the boats as the competition became more fierce, but there were different sorts of casualties in the classes above us. The change became noticeable the following year when our class first contended for the varsity.

The wind that fought the current almost every spring afternoon had died away. Darkness was falling. Soon Tony's spotlight would reflect upon the glassy smoothness, but perhaps not. The workout, after all, was nearly over. Lights from the boathouse stood out clearly when I turned my head. I caught the high-pitched whine of the novice women's coxswain remonstrating with her charges for banging their old Pocock against the dock. The lightweights were at the finish line, rotating their boats in the darkness to dock against the current. Wraithlike in our gray Carbocraft, we drifted from the thousand-meter mark toward seven fifty. I had imagined one last three-minute piece to finish the day, but the passing outline of the swim club signified only two more minutes. Tony would not turn us back upriver. In the darkness it was too dangerous; besides, the women's varsity were coming down. Just one more piece.

I was at the limit of my endurance. We were all at the limit. Still, it was Wednesday, and on Saturday we would race Penn. That first year in the varsity, I was more frightened of Penn than Harvard. Penn had beaten my freshman boat twice. Penn's varsity had beaten Yale for the past thirteen years. No one but our ageless boatman even remembered what the Blackwell Cup looked like, it had been so long. And Penn had Otto at their six seat—my seat. Otto was awesome. I had never seen him but I knew he was enormous: 6 feet 6 of blond, blue-eyed Prussian, the strongest man on the U.S. national team and only a junior. Otto was one of the few names that had stuck in my two years of rowing. His real name was Phil but that didn't describe the aura. Otto!

Otto was Pete's elder brother. Rowing at seven, Pete was in his first year in our varsity, but he had not had such an illustrious career as an oarsman. At the Ferry his freshman year, he had been cut from the first to the second boat. That night he had fled, leaving nothing but a note to say that it was over.

Pete faded from the crew as fast as he left it. My freshman year, I never heard of him. I don't think anyone bore him any malice. *Il n'exista plus.* He was gone. Whatever the year's effort had gained him with his fellows might just as well not have happened.

He stayed away from rowing that year; my sophomore year, however, he was back. Shy and painfully deter-mined, he rarely shared his dreams of making the var-sity. I did not know his story, but as he was Otto's brother, I thought his dreams would be fulfilled.

Otto's brother gained a lot of respect in the fall and winter from his classmates. I guess I should say he re-

gained a lot of respect. His boats did well. He was conscientious, strong and determined—a contender for the
first boat.

In Florida the work paid off. Pete earned the seven
seat of the varsity, and we won the first two races easily.
During the next week Pete was moved to the junior
varsity. The decision had been close, and it looked as
though it would be reversed. I assumed that the closer
we got to the Penn race, the more competitive Pete
would become. The chance to race his brother would
bring out everything Pete had.

During that last hard practice before Penn, Pete was
back in the varsity for what I assumed was his last chance
to prove himself, and despite a pain in his stomach, he
was moving the boat well. It was the last piece of the
day, the last hard work before Penn, and his last chance
to make the boat for the race. "Let's kill them this time,"
I whispered forward. "This is for your seat!"

"Tony! I can't do it." Pete did not even look around
as he yelled to the launch. Holding his stomach, he called
again. Silently we paddled in.

There had been times when for one reason or another
I had not been able to pull. It happened occasionally to
every oarsman. "Grit your teeth and pull half pressure!"
was the standard response. No one was fooled for long
but nothing would be said. The only person I remember
who was unable to complete a practice was our captain,
who was taken from the boat after a long piece in Florida. That night he had been flown back to New Haven
for hernia surgery. I hoped Pete had something as dramatic.

Paddling in those last few minutes marked the end
of our friendship. I didn't doubt that something was
wrong with his stomach—but I don't think I really

cared. We had all had times when we should have stopped. Dave Potter hurt his back and stupidly kept on rowing. Potter could stroke any boat he wanted because we knew he would never give up.

I wanted to say to Pete, "It's all right. Pull yourself together and you will be given another chance." In rowing there is always another chance. One can keep rowing year after year and the program will create a place. But not so the oarsmen.

I remember watching the remains of a Formula One race car being hauled out of a ditch at Laguna Seca, a Can-Am course in California. "What happened?" I asked.

The aged timer looked wistful, and said with sadness and respect, "He tried the turn as hard as he could, but halfway through, he ran out of talent." At least he found his limit.

The next day Ted rejoined the boat and we prepared to race Penn. Penn had beaten Harvard a year before. Penn had Otto. Penn had not lost to Yale in thirteen years. Those facts rang through my brain as Penn moved back. They took us by a length on the start, we pulled even by one thousand meters and were a length ahead after fifteen hundred. Through the last fifty strokes Penn and Otto were moving every stroke. They came inch by inch, but Andy did not call up the rating for fear of upsetting the boat, of breaking our concentration. So long as there was no hesitation, Penn would not catch us. Had the racecourse been twenty meters longer, we would have lost. I came home with Otto's shirt, the hardest prize I had ever won. The junior varsity lost.

That Saturday afternoon in late April, 1978, was the death of the Penn crew and the revival of Yale. Penn was shattered. Unable to rebound from the loss, they were crushed by Harvard the next week and then failed to make the six-boat final at the Eastern Sprints. Yale rested the next week in preparation for that first Sprints victory in twenty years; but Yale also lost something. Those not riding our new wave of triumph were drowned by it. Success became established as the only hierarchy. More than ever before, friendship, even identity, had to be proven on the water.

Henley

"We're number one! We're number one!" Cal Berkeley's varsity chanted after beating Washington at the Pacific-10 championship May 20, 1979, only one week after we won the Eastern Championships and three weeks before the Race. A Cal oarsman explained the outburst to *Sports Illustrated*.

"We haven't rowed Yale yet, but at the San Diego in April we beat everyone except Harvard—Washington, Syracuse, Northeastern, Penn, all of them. And last week Harvard got creamed by Yale at the Eastern Sprints."

"If you're number one, then what about Yale? They are still undefeated."

"We'll beat them at Henley in July," he replied. That would decide it, the national championship.

A few days after we read that issue of *Sports Illustrated*, Steve Gladstone, Cal's coach, received a "Peanuts" cartoon in the mail. It depicted Lucy in the outfield with her baseball glove, chanting "We're number one! We're number one!" Then from nowhere came a baseball that bonked her on the top of the head. Picking herself off the ground, Lucy muttered, "Well, I thought we were number one." To her baseball cap had been added a golden California *C* while the ball now sported a large blue *Y*. Cal orsmen were not too good at logic, but we figured that they would understand who really was number one. The cartoon did not arrive in California until the day after we lost to Harvard.

There is an intercollegiate national championship regatta, the IRA at Syracuse, but because of conflicting race schedules the top crews, including Yale, Harvard, Washington and California, usually did not attend—preferring instead to arrange their own championships. The Henley Royal Regatta in England was the most enticing way of solving the problem.

Henley is the ultimate prize for American college crews. It is the most exciting kind of two-boat racing, combined with the pagentry of nineteenth-century England. What Wimbledon is to tennis and the Ascot is to horse racing, Henley is that and more to rowing. After winning the Sprints we counted on a trip to Henley to race California, the West Coast champions, but losing to Harvard left us uncertain. We were still the only undefeated crew in the country over a 2,000-meter course, and as such we could not let California's blitherings go unchallenged, but could we in good conscience go to Henley after losing to Harvard?

Since freshman year I had dreamed of the trip; in fact, each year we had expected to go. As freshmen we had beaten Harvard but were told that the alumni would send us only if we won our final race at Syracuse. Bad conditions and a poorly rowed race sent us home. The

141

next year we won the Sprints, but because we lost to Dartmouth, we decided to wait until after the Harvard race to decide about Henley. When we lost, the alumni, who had been gathering money for our trip, were so annoyed that they helped send our freshmen instead.

The night after the Race in 1979 as I drove back to Karen's apartment, I thought that we should again forgo Henley, that I should quit rowing and do something else. But I soon realized that the only kinship I had was with my boat. I awakened the next morning to that kick in the stomach, the nausea of knowing that it was all over, but there was a difference from 1978. Even in defeat there was no question but that we had raced the race of our lives. Never had our limits been pushed so far. I wanted only to get back in the boat—to see just how much farther we could go. Despite jobs and family that awaited us, there was no question that we had to go on. Harvard, I found out later, would have gone to Henley if they had beaten us in the Sprints.

That same morning I received a letter from my sister at Oxford which gave directions to the Yale Club of London's special pavilion at Henley. Someone, I realized, had decided well in advance of the Harvard race that the Yale crew would compete at Henley. In fact, by June 23, only thirteen days after racing Harvard, we were at the town of Henley-on-Thames, preparing to race first at a regatta in Nottingham and then to return for the Royal Regatta.

The town of Henley-on-Thames is secluded in the gently rolling countryside between Oxford and London. The pleasure boats lining the Thames set the pace of life, remaining moored along the grassy banks except on the rare occasions when social calls become absolutely necessary. The regatta is the town's garden party. With no publicity other than 150 years of tradition, more than a hundred thousand attend. The crowds of Wimbledon, bored with the confinement of the grandstands, dust off their crew blazers and straw boaters and relocate along the bank of the Thames. Once the regatta was fully under way, I was to feel foolish hitching a ride from our inn outside of town to the racecourse. "So obviously American," I chided myself in my best British accent. But what the hell, I was American, and so long as we won, who cared? Decorum redefined, I stuck out a thumb. Instantly an automobile halted before me, from which an elderly gentleman opened the window and inquired if I was an oarsman. I was dressed the part with my blue Yale blazer and white duck trousers, but almost before I had time to reply, the chauffeur was out and ushering me into the car. Never before had I been in a Rolls-Royce.

When we arrived, the months of preparation for the regatta were almost finished. The flowers and smaller ornaments would not be arranged until the day before the first race, but the racecourse had been set, the pavilions were standing and the enclosures were in order. At Henley most of the original class distinctions of the 150-year-old regatta are still maintained. To mingle with the old-school gentlemen who would stroll beside their ladies inside the Steward's Enclosure was very expensive for the four days of racing—although a glimpse at the pavilions, laden with strawberries, pastries and champagne, would convince anyone that being there was worth the price. To sit in the covered grandstands within the Enclosure took a dispensation from the Queen. Fifty years ago Henley's decorum prevented Jack Kelly, the U.S. champion single sculler and the father of Princess Grace, from racing the Diamond Sculls because he had once worked as a bricklayer. Kelly, the owner of a brick-works in Philadelphia, responded by packaging a prime specimen from his factory and sending it to the Queen. Years later, Kelly's son returned to Henley, where he won that prestigious single sculling trophy, and created the legendary "KELLY FOR BRICKWORK" T-shirts that were still being worn in Philadelphia boathouses.

Henley is in fact so proper that the British, who will give odds on anything from Wimbledon to Ascot to the Oxford-Cambridge boat race, will not give odds on Henley. On the banks of the course itself, gentlemen have been known to wager on individual races, but all betting is carefully out of reach of the mob. Unlike Wimbledon or Ascot, Henley is not televised and only vaguely mentioned in the London papers. *The New York Times* has better coverage of Henley than any of the British papers.

I learned what an exclusive society Henley is from the dean of Calhoun College at Yale, who happened to arrive in England during the middle of the regatta and wanted to come watch. He found nothing in the papers about what was happening at Henley so he called the local gambling house to see what the bookies could tell him. The bookie told him no—that there were no odds given or bets taken, and he didn't know the schedule. Disconsolately, the dean boarded the next train to Henley to find out for himself.

Ex-oarsmen returning to Henley were readily identifiable. Even if one is not wearing the traditional white duck trousers and blazers, the bearing and the special gleam that return for those few days each year are unmistakable. The dean recognized the elderly gentleman seated next to him as an oarsman making the pilgrimage so he engaged him in conversation.

"Tell me, sir, are you bound for the races?"

At length the man nodded and said something to the effect that he had rowed in the Grand Challenge Cup forty-two years earlier and had managed to be back every year, "except during the war, of course." So the dean outlined his attempts to find information about the race and asked why there was so little publicity.

"Too many people as it is," the gentleman replied. "Quite a few good ones but a lot of chaff. To put it in the papers would be to invite the mob; after all, they have already got Wimbledon."

Beyond the Enclosure, a towpath follows the Thames downstream to the starting line. As I walked from the finish line along the towpath, the enclosures gave way to estates, which in turn gave way to pastures. The pavilions diminished into glorified concession stands, but during the races the crowds maintained an atmosphere of civility and humor unmatched at any other athletic event I have attended. In that week before the races began, however, the towpath was empty except for occasional strafing by coaches following their crews on bicycles. They rode at the edge of the river, keeping pace with their shells, scolding their crews through electric bullhorns while alternately clicking a stopwatch for stroke cadences and ringing those damned little bells like those mounted on every kid's tricycle. Upon hearing the dreadful peals, pedestrians would dive for the trenches. No protocol directed coaches traveling in opposite directions. Englishmen approaching each other went left. When an Englishman approached a coach of any other nationality, he still went left, but the other went right and both ended swearing, if not subaqueous.

The racecourse looked the aquatic equivalent of a medieval jousting arena. It was 80 feet wide and 1⅜ miles long (twenty strokes longer than a 2,000-meter course). A small island with a white house marked the start. Stretching away from the island, white posts at twenty-yard intervals marked the course as if a picket fence had been intended. Floating log booms connected the posts to damp outside wakes and provided mooring for the fleets of punts loaded with spectators. Racing on the course was a tremendous test of concentration. Only about ten feet separate the oars of the two boats racing down the course; no more than that separates each boat from the log boom. From the spectators' vantage, the beauty of the course is that it is only about twenty feet from the bank. Not only is the view spectacular, but the commands of the coxswains are as clear to the audience and to the opposition as they are to the intended oarsmen. The boats race two at a time. The winner will climb the ladder toward the finals and the loser will join the hundred thousand spectators on the bank.

Before we left the States I had wondered how we would find a boat to row, but I learned at Henley that Tony had ordered a new Carbocraft the year before—for delivery in England that June. He too had made plans early to be at Henley. The sleek blue carbon fiber shell was already in the boat tent when we arrived. It would take a few practices to adjust to the new boat, but that also gave us time to recover from the time change and to become familiar with our surroundings. Our first practice in England and our first time on the Henley course, Tony advised us to just paddle along and stop often to enjoy the scenery.

Exuberantly we paddled past the houses on the far side of the river to the finish line at the edge of the Enclosure. At the finish line we entered the practice lane and headed toward the starting line. It then took about fifteen minutes to paddle the length of the course to the start. On the way we glanced from side to side and waved to those on the bank. We were too much in awe of the surroundings even to try to look impressive. At the start, we rounded the island and turned back to row between the log booms on the course itself. Never before had I rowed on such a narrow course. Each stroke I imagined that the blade would hit a log and catapult me into the river.

Tony had told us to take special notice of those landmarks which the announcer would later use to call the relative positions of the boats. The first point was the end of the island, twenty strokes into the race. The next mark was the Barrier, about two minutes into the race, and the third mark was Fawley, the halfway marker. The British believed that whichever boat was ahead at the Barrier would win the race, so they often raced for an early lead and then tried to hang on. The record book gives the fastest times to both the Barrier and Fawley, tempting some crews to sprint off the line in the hope of a record time to one of these markers. Such crews generally collapse two or three minutes into the race, but it is not necessary to win to set a record.

When I think of Henley, I think of the easy, joyous formality and how well Yale seemed to fit, but during our first days in England that impression was far from the truth. We drove to Henley from Heathrow Airport with twenty oarsmen, two coxswains, the coach, boatman, manager, twenty oars and all of our bags stuffed into two rented vans. Boisterous and belligerent, we hit Henley with the stately aplomb of a charging rhinoceros. We were ready to race, but it was not a readiness that could have been contained within the formal splendor of Henley. Henley was a prize, not a grudge match, yet guilt from the Harvard race cast one shadow and anxiety about California cast another, darkening the prospect of Henley's pageant. Fortunately, the race at Nottingham, one week before the Royal Regatta, gave us a chance to leave Henley for a few days to race California on less splendid grounds. The winners would return to Henley knowing that they had earned the right to enjoy it.

The Nottinghamshire International Regatta is one of the first international regattas of the season, giving national teams a chance to test themselves well before the World Championships. In the previous few years, East Germany, Russia and Bulgaria had won the Guinness Cup for championship eights. In 1979 the only national teams were the Czechoslovakians and the British lightweights. California was the only crew I cared about.

The course at Nottingham is essentially a 2,000-meter swimming pool, built for the World Rowing Championships in 1975. Like a swimming pool the rectangle is divided into six lanes, using six-inch-in-diameter circular buoys spaced at five-meter intervals. The start seems like the start of a backstroke race. The oarsmen hunch forward, facing the start, while the stern of the shell is held against the wall of the pool by an aligner crouched on the starting platform. The platforms and aligners allow boats to be perfectly even at the start. At the finish line is a five-story steel and glass tower erected to help determine the closest of photo finishes. Even the spectators are accounted for. At the edge of the pool is a roadway on which a flatbed truck with bleachers follows each race. At the finish line an electric scoreboard provides times and relative positions every five hundred meters of the race.

It all looks impressive but the designers were too clever. The plain around Nottingham affords no respite from the constant and unpleasantly cold wind, but rather than simply building a windbreak, the designers planned to make use of the powerful force. Figuring that a rowing course could double as a sailing facility, they rotated the axis of the pool to create a constant crosswind. A small ridge shelters the first two lanes and a line of pine trees shelters the others for a few hundred meters, but generally the wind sweeps across unchecked. When the afternoon wind kicks up, lanes one and two remain flat while the outside lanes get increasingly un-rowable. As a result, the exact placement of the lanes, starting blocks and judges' tower make the races no more exact and probably less fair than the practice races we rowed every Friday in New Haven.

Seeing the course for the first time, we laughed until told that we had drawn lane six. Czechoslovakia in lane five separated us from California in lane four. The British lightweight team was in lane three. The flattest water in lanes one and two was unused. Lane four, we figured, would be worth six or eight seconds' advantage over the 2,000 meters. The wind meant settling the national sprint championship from the equivalent of two lengths behind.

"*Yale, prêt.*" The French of the international starting procedure was muffled in the wind. "*Tchécoslovaquie, prêt.*"

"*Attention!*" The Czech bow had blown off target. Each boat had to be declared *prêt* before the race could begin. The coxswain signifies being ready by lowering his hand. If a coxswain's hand is raised, the procedure halts. The Czech coxswain held his hand in the air as the port side paddled to swing the boat back into the wind. The trick was to keep the bow pointed far enough into the wind so that when the final commands started, there would be just enough time for the bow to drift back in line.

"*Tchécoslovaquie, prêt!*"

Our bow was blown back toward the shore and Andy raised his hand.

"*Attention!*" I relaxed while Joe, in the two seat, pulled us around. Andy lowered his hand.

"*Yale, prêt...Tchécoslovaquie, prêt...California, prêt.*"

"*Attention!*"

The stern of the Cal boat had drifted out of the aligner's hands. Rapidly losing patience, the starter, with his thick British accent, chastised Cal in French. That no one in the race spoke French neither helped the situation nor altered the rules of international competition. Cal meanwhile tangled oars with the Czechs, who gesticulated wildly. Translation was unnecessary.

Huddled against the wind, I thought of my sweat shirt lying warm and dry on the dock. I had anticipated a quick race. In any case, sweat shirts were constricting and added unnecessary weight to the boat. No one else had showed the same conscience so I had felt especially virtuous, but the previous race had taken half an hour to align the boats. Unable to move onto the course for fear of blocking the race, we just sat. Wearing only a wet T-shirt and shorts, I soon began to shake uncontrollably. After about twenty minutes Tony, who had been riding alongside the course on a bicycle, noticed that I looked very cold and lent me his jacket from the 1968 Olympic games. I wore it until we went to the line and then wrapped it around my feet. I considered leaving it on, but couldn't. I had not earned the right to wear such a jacket in the first place. I certainly could not race in it. I wonder now if the cold had made me so stupid. With each delay it became harder to hang onto the oar.

"*Tchécoslovaquie, prêt!....California, prêt.*"

Shivering, I looked over at the Czechs. Even they looked unhappy. Once again our bow blew toward the rocks and Andy raised his hand. I resumed thinking about how cold it was, believing that the starter would begin again.

"*Êtes-vous prêts....*"

We lunged up the slide to the ready position, our bow still aimed at the rocks.

"*Partez!*"

Careering toward shore with the rudder spraying water like a water ski, I tensed my body for the collision. Having seen an oarsman catapulted from a shell when his blade hit a bridge on the Charles, I almost stopped rowing. I realized, however, that if we hit the rocks, we would have to start the race all over again. I kept jamming my legs down until we were clear.

In every race there was the conscious decision to pull to win or perhaps not to. At any moment it seemed that the boat would decide that losing was not that painful. I was cold and sick of racing. The conditions were so blatantly unfair that rowing hardly seemed worthwhile. Cal had disappeared. With a straight start in much flatter water, they moved ahead by two lengths in the first two hundred meters. Czechoslovakia was only a little ahead but they were a national team. The Bulgarians had won last year, the Russians a few years before that. Yale did not fit the list.

A wave broke over the gunwale, dousing my shorts, as the bow swung back around. The sudden chill riveted my eyes downward, focusing then on the USA jacket at my feet. I wanted one of those jackets. It seemed to me bad enough that I had worn the jacket without earning it, but it was reprehensible to put it on and then lose heart. Angrily, and with a trace of fear, I began to pull.

In a mile and a quarter of water and wind, any number of things can happen to the advantage of one boat or the other. Headwinds help some boats, tailwinds help others. Some crews are demoralized by rough water but others can't row aggressively without the added recklessness of water crashing over the riggers. At one regatta that I watched at Princeton, every winning crew was in lane one and every losing crew was in lane five, simply because lane one was sheltered from the cross-headwind. At Nottingham there were any number of similar reasons to lose the race, and for the first five hundred meters I believed that it had been lost before we had even started, but another thought repeated itself in my mind. The California papers, my home papers, would give about an inch of one column to this event. That inch would be room enough to name the victor and the margin of victory—nothing more. With so much pride riding on what would be said in that column, knowing why we lost would be little consolation. Victory and the margin of victory became the only truth, the complete story.

We pulled desperately back toward California, our speed checked every few strokes by the crash of another wave over the riggers, but there was a chance. The line of trees would give us flat water. I imagined what Harvard must have felt moving back through us two weeks before. They had hung on, a length behind, waiting for the two-mile mark just as we now waited for the trees. Cal was not as good as we. They were not as good as Harvard. A sudden surge might demoralize them. The Czechs were even with us but, as Andy reminded us, they were going nowhere.

The wind stopped as we came in line with the trees. Our boat, which had been canted over to port, righted itself. The riggers no longer hit water. Oftentimes a change, even a change for the better, upsets the rhythm; however, in the next five hundred meters we gained every stroke, moving through California. "This is the national championship and I've got their bow ball!" screamed Andy. The Czechs had fallen back by half a length.

Back in the rough water for the last few hundred meters, we increased our lead. Once the boat swings correctly, it is easier to keep it moving, and we knew that California was in trouble. Racing with all the advantages and then being passed had ruined their concentration. As their stroke lost control of his oar a plume of water conceded defeat, awakening us to the fact that we were racing the Czechs, not California. They were coming up fast. Desperately we cranked up the stroke rating to 38. With twenty strokes to go, Andy called the rating up two more strokes. Ten strokes later he called it up two more. The rhythm was breaking. Last five! "Easy!" The Czechs finished less than a second behind, wondering how a university could beat a national team.

That night I discovered that British boathouses were different from American. The facilities for the boats themselves were similar. A boat bay is a boat bay; but the British houses had no showers or changing rooms. Such conveniences would cut into the space of the bar and dance floor. We climbed the steep and rickety stairway leading from the street and opened the door into a myriad of flashing lights and people dancing. A British oarsman who I recognized from the race charged over, handed me a beer, and went back to dancing. I introduced myself to a woman from a Belfast crew and followed his example.

Yale returned to Henley with a sense of belonging.

By beating California and Czechoslovakia we both assured ourselves that we were the fastest college in the
United States and proved that we were of international
caliber. The brightly colored boat tents, the elaborate
decorations, and the course itself each had a special
meaning for us. Along with Oxford, California and the
British National Team, we had the honor of rowing for
the Grand Challenge cup, the most prestigious event.

On our return to Henley, however, I noticed a change
in my attitude. Tony brought us to England for good
racing. He seemed to expect us to divorce ourselves from
the surroundings and gird ourselves as we had for all
our other races. I had wanted to beat California, to silence them, and I still wanted to win at Henley, but at
the same time, something inside rebelled against maintaining that grudge. Henley seemed not a place to prove
oneself, but to enjoy the success of just being there.
Honor had demanded that we face California, but I was
not at all dismayed when fate determined that we would
not have to race them again. In the semifinals we would
race Oxford, and California would race (and surely lose
to) the British national team.

The tents that had been empty when we left were
nearly full. Hundreds of shells were now stacked together on the racks in preparation for the four days of
racing that would begin Thursday. Up to forty boats
competed in each of the eight challenge cups, but because there were only four entries in the Grand Challenge, we would not race until the semifinals against
Oxford on Saturday. During the week we practiced
lightly and lounged about the river, watching the early
elimination races and the coaches on the towpath.

Henley: that wonderful dreamland of billowing pavilions, clear sunny days, shells gliding and lovely women

on one arm; parading through the crowds as a Grand Oarsman with a *Y* and crossed oars emblazoned on my blue blazer. The thrill of racing seemed insignificant beside the pure joy of being, of participating in such a splendid pageant.

I dozed in the sunshine, my coat and tie having found usefulness as a pillow and a bookmark. My sister had bicycled from Oxford that morning to report that the Oxford Blue Boat would be little competition. They had not rowed together seriously in more than a month. Thinking of how devastating a few months off would be to our boat, I laughed. The Oxford crew was also small, averaging little more than 6 feet and less than 180 pounds. After my sister had left, the Oxford stroke arrived. He sounded so cocky that I gave him a tour of our boat, introducing him to the size 17 shoes mounted for our seven man. Half of his leg would have fit into those shoes. He left, looking shaken. Well satisfied, I wandered down the course for my nap.

When I awakened, a woman was seated close beside me on the grass. She did not appear interested in my awakening, but she seemed so familiar. Enthralled, I kept glancing back, trying to place her. I noticed then we were both reading the same novel. "Like the book?" I asked eventually.

"Pardon me?"

"Anne!" The woman I had danced with at Nottingham—looking much different from how I had remembered her, but I could not have forgotten the voice. She smiled as if to say, "What took you so long?" There are no women's races at Henley, but her crew was staying close by, training for the races in Lucerne. Together we lounged on the grass, watching the races. We both cheered when the Yale junior varsity passed by ahead of Cambridge and hugged when they won—vicarious racing at its best. Somehow in the excitement we never let go. The magic that was Henley became complete.

Appropriately, Henley was to be the scene of our toughest competition; in fact, the *Daily Telegraph* predicted that we would be thrashed by Oxford and never get to row against the British national team, but the *Telegraph* had also predicted that we would lose to Czechoslovakia. Oxford did give us a scare in the beginning of the race by sprinting from the starting line. In the first ten strokes they gained a seat length every stroke, and we had what I thought was one of our faster starts, but by the Barrier they ran out of steam. The *Telegraph* barely reported our victory but had no doubt that we would be thrashed by the British. I must admit that the *Telegraph* was not alone in that prediction.

Only three weeks earlier the British team had finished one second behind the world champion East Germans, a fact which I conveniently had been able to ignore until I watched the British humiliate California by eight lengths—but hubris was returning. For the first time, we had nothing to lose. We would row higher and harder, removing all stops, to see if we could last. It was a race to test our old limits. I had Anne's scarf to carry in the tournament.

I was happy when we backed the boat into the start beside the British boat. My pulse was high, my body was prepared, yet I was happy. I felt no fear. Eric's back seemed tremendous, and in fact all of us had grown larger since we entered the shell. There were a hundred thousand people on the bank, yet I don't remember any sound. There were just our eight and the British. We wished each other luck, and meant it.

"Are you ready? Go!"

Had the British beaten us off the line as Oxford had, the race might have become impossible. After watching California's humiliation, we must have all known in the backs of our minds that we might be embarrassed, but ten strokes into the race we were in front. I looked across and was even with the bowman of the British boat. Four seats up. At the end of the island, they settled to 42 strokes a minute and we were 38—three seats up. By the Barrier, a third of the way down the course, the British led by several seats, but when they dropped their cadence to 39 strokes per minute, it was our turn to move. How glorious it was to be moving back toward the British national team! Ten strokes later, the British again raised their rating to over 40 strokes per minute and halted our move. By Fawley, the halfway point, they were a length ahead and finally moved to two lengths. I gave myself, convinced that we could win, but when it was obvious that we would not, I felt no temptation to slack off. The boat was swinging, the brass band saluted. Every muscle sang with the boat. Harmony in motion.

I gave myself, knowing that whatever the outcome Anne would be on the dock. Enraptured by the same vitality we would unite. The crashing of oars giving way to the crushing of cotton. To explore each other in the moonlight as reflections of sunrises on the river condensed in sinew. In the morning we would return to our crews, she to complete the European rowing circuit, and I to Dartmouth and the selection camp for the U.S. National Rowing Team.

The Set

Im Anfang war die Tat.
In the beginning was the deed.

"Deeds were never invented, they were done," argues Jung. "Thoughts, on the other hand, are a relatively late discovery of man." The word itself has in Western civilization only recently been separated from the act. Words, thoughts and deeds are inextricably mixed within our psyches. "What we call civilized consciousness has steadily separated itself from the basic instincts, but those instincts have not disappeared."

Why then did athletics, the perfection of the act, come to be thought of as mundane and degrading, as separate from intellect and spirit? In his classic work on Greek culture, *Paideia,* Werner Jaeger pinpoints the occasion of the first split. It was the middle of the sixth century

158

B.C. The old athletic system, aristocratic and amateur, had ended. Under the ever-increasing emphasis on winning, the great games at Olympia and Delphi, Nemea and the Corinthian Isthmus had fallen prey to rampant professionalism.

> ...Only then did Xenophanes' attack on the overestimation of the coarse unintellectual "strength of the body" call forth a late but lasting echo. As soon as the Greeks began to feel that the spirit was different from or even hostile to the body, the old athletic ideal was degraded beyond hope of salvation, and at once loses its important position in Greek life, although athletics survived centuries more as mere sport. Originally, nothing could have been more foreign to it than the purely intellectual conception of physical strength or efficiency. The ideal unity of physical and spiritual which although it is irreparably lost to us we still admire in the masterpieces of Greek sculpture, indicates how we must understand the athletic ideal of manly prowess, even if that ideal may have been very far from reality.

Codifying Xenophanes' subjugation of the athletic to the intellectual, Aristotle defined man's particular realm of excellence as his capacity to reason. Reason, he argued, is the quality of mankind that separates us from other forms of life. Since then, thinking men have almost invariably put pure thought ahead of physical pursuits—as I did before becoming obsessed by crew. Having now lived in both worlds, as an intellectual and as an athlete, I wonder if there is indeed a hierarchy.

In the fifth century B.C., Athens and Sparta were the most powerful Greek city-states. Athens was the center of culture, gaining power from her navy and commercial fleet, while Sparta was the land of great armies and raw physicality. The two cities despised each other, but they were such opposites that neither could mortally damage the other. The Athenians ruled the seas but fled before the Spartan army; likewise, the Spartans laid waste to the Athenian countryside but could not hurt the city, which was supplied from the sea. Together Athens and Sparta had smashed the Persians, but as opponents they bled each other into stalemated ruin.

The two cities were once equals, yet in Sparta today there is nothing left—nothing to lend Sparta any distinction beside the splendid ruins of ancient Athens; however, even in her most powerful years Sparta appeared little more than a battle camp. Thucydides, the historian who chronicled the wars between Athens and Sparta, correctly predicted that the remains of Athens would lead future scholars to believe that Athens was ten times more powerful than she actually was, while the remains of Sparta would make her appear ten times less significant. The writings of Thucydides, the Athenian, are in fact the major reason we appreciate the glory of Sparta.

From our present perspective, one look at Athens is enough to convince us that she was the greater city. After two thousand years, she still lives in our culture; but would it have bothered the Spartans not to be remembered? Sparta, like Athens, created her own destiny. Each became the best of what she attempted. Remember that both Athens and Sparta had large slave populations whose labor allowed the citizens to concentrate on other tasks than their own subsistence. In Athens, slave labor allowed for the flowering of culture; but in Sparta, being freed from menial labor allowed the men to train constantly for battle. Male children were separated from their families at age seven to begin training as warriors. The Spartan system did not adapt and was therefore destroyed; however, the Spartans were slow to change, because although the world around them was changing, the fundamental nature of man as they viewed him was not changing at all. The Spartans were not dumb jocks. They lived as athletes, excelling in the present without thought for the past or future.

The Spartan way of life: living with men in isolated camps ordered by a rigid hierarchy of age and strength; waking early to train all day in an unproductive enterprise while others provide subsistence; a rigorous, demanding life without culture, art or love, but with fraternity, dignity, prestige and most of all a goal. It seems so foreign, and to most people it probably is foreign. Gales Ferry is a Spartan camp and there I spent some of the most rewarding and pleasant moments of my life. It is still an expensive life to maintain—but as it was two thousand years ago, there are those who would give anything not to see it vanish.

Athletic ideals vanished altogether in the Middle Ages because there was no room for individual achievement. Athletics glorify the individual and the species, not the Creator. Just as sculpture disappeared after the fall of the Romans and had to be reborn hundreds of years later, from Romanesque reliefs to Renaissance free-standing forms, so too did athletics have to be reborn.

By providing a path toward an attainable perfection, modern athletics provide a security of personal ability, a worship of the human form and human potentiality—a sign of independence; but athletics can be the despair of anything beyond the individual. The perfection is unavoidably linked to the most unbearable source of human insecurity. The marvels of the body are short-lived, reminding us of our own mortality. Becoming an athlete is then the building of a new self-confidence, a

161

confidence exclaiming to the world that this body can withstand anything the world has to offer, but which can only briefly cover up the real sources of insecurity.

Paul Weiss, the first modern philosopher to look at sports, argued:

> ...[The athlete] does not take account of realities that may have much to do with his present and eventual welfare. Sport is a transient source of excellence. One in which the young have the easiest grasp of things beyond themselves, but which should give way to more serious pursuit.

The recent literature on running however, denies this transience. Running, it is argued, brings one in contact with a reality which transcends the everyday and is therefore more real than the everyday. Running in particular and athletics in general have become quasi-mystical, quick access routes to salvation.

Growing up in California during the sixties and seventies, I came in contact with a large number of quick access routes, some at first hand and some through my parents. I cannot condemn any of them, from running to meditation, but I do know that people who really dedicate themselves to such pursuits (and such people are rare) go the way of the Spartans—the world of pure present.

I row because it provides me with a sense of identity. More than that, rowing provides an objective framework against which to measure myself: a definite goal, an attainable perfection; a ritual removing me from the seemingly random vacillations of outside reality. The intellectual damns me for being unwilling to cope with the real world, but he is wrong. The goal is not that sport give way to serious pursuit, nor is it that we should all take up jogging. The athletic ideal is in the world of the present, while the "serious pursuits" are spread through the past and future. The goal should be the synthesis of the two: the present and the future, the finite and the infinite. Werner Jaeger is also wrong. The ideal unity of the physical and the spiritual is no longer irreparably lost to us. At Gales Ferry I did not think that it was far out of reach. I could not live at the Ferry all my life, but I feared graduation when I could not return.

Michael Novak in *The Joy of Sports* tries to develop a synthesis of what I call the Spartan and the Athenian for the spectator. With the distance of the spectator, he argues, sports achieve metaphorical and allegorical significance. The human condition can be mirrored in a single race—a Greek tragedy inspired on the river for the interpretation of the fans. Within a limited framework the spectator can achieve this synthesis. For example, for the Old Blues on the bank at New London, defeat becomes a metaphorical death. But this is only the parable of the spectator. As an athlete, I see the fan—not the loser—as the victim. The fan submerges himself in the spectacle but he can no more affect it than he can alter the lines of a play.

From the river, such allegories fail. If a race is rowed poorly, then losing is demoralizing but not fatal. If a race is rowed well, to call defeat death is to be blind to all that created it. Too much life goes into the act of competing.

As a competitor, winner or loser, one crosses the line into limbo. The adrenaline is gone, the anticipation is gone. The verdict is either comforting or devastating but it neither returns the exhilaration of the race nor helps directly to win the next. Maybe all that matters is that there is a next.

Musical Boats

Tragic heroes, mythic heroes, antiheroes: I was introduced to them on the lawn of my high school's English center where my brother's and sister's friends and I read to one another. I was then 165 pounds, with glasses, braces and acne. That was before I played football. That was also when I believed in literature. Life copied art, or at least tried to.

In those days I was taken by Cyrano de Bergerac. "What would you have me do?" he asked. "Seek for the patronage of some great man and like a creeping vine on a tall tree climb upward where I cannot stand alone? No, thank you!" I will be like he was, I had thought to myself.

By chance I reread Cyrano on the plane back from Henley. I supposed I was a lot closer to Cyrano than I had been in high school. I felt that I had pushed about as hard as my soul would allow for excellence in one small facet of being human. I was learning to push harder. But to me the athletic consciousness was not Cyrano's "Know thyself"; it was, as Clint Eastwood said in *Dirty Harry,* "A man must know his limitations."

By the time the Yale eight returned from Henley, we had progressed as far as we were going to. When people asked about the Harvard race, there would be the pain of remembrance, but we had learned so much about each other and about our capabilities as a crew that we could almost smile when we shrugged our shoulders. Years ago, when the U.S. National Rowing Team (the team that rows in the World Championships and the Olympics) was chosen each year by trials races, our eight would have stayed together to race against the best clubs and universities for the right to represent the United States in the World Championships. Since 1972, however, most national team oarsmen have been selected individually. As an eight our season was finished, but we did not stop. For a variety of reasons, some of which I did not understand, the Yale eight-minus-one decided individually to attend selection camp for the national team. Andy Messer, our six man, left for the Canadian team camp directly from Henley.

The 1979 World Championships were scheduled for September 5–8 in Bled, a lake resort in the mountains of Slovenia, Yugoslavia. The selection camp began July 16, 1979, at Dartmouth, five days after our return from Henley. Harry Parker from Harvard was to coach the eight, and Steve Gladstone from Cal Berkeley would coach the four-with-coxswain. Other boats like the pair-with-coxswain and the four-without would be chosen by trials races after the camp.

The camp was for us an opportunity to kill the remainder of the summer in double workouts against legendary rowing heroes to discover how we measured against the Ottos of the rowing world—and a chance to discover who Harry was after our loss at the Ferry. None of us had been to a national selection camp before; in fact, only a few Yale oarsmen had ever been through the process, so we did not know what to expect. We did know that Harry Parker expected sixty or eighty oarsmen, from which he would choose an eight, a four-with-coxswain and two spare oarsmen. Fourteen oarsmen and two coxswains. We came together, but few if any of us would make the team.

Eric and John were the favored pair from Yale. John expected to make the eight. Eric was as self-effacing as ever. Matthew and Karl were only sophomores. Neither was as strong as Eric, and I don't think they took the camp so seriously as we three juniors. For Joe and Ted, the real world was closing in. Joe was to start Cornell Medical School and Ted had a job with an investment bank in New York. With only a few more weeks of freedom, I doubted that they were completely serious about the camp. To be cut from the camp would be to have been found wanting. Still, not to go at all would have meant being left behind.

I drove from New Haven to Dartmouth with our coxswain, Andy Fisher. Andy had kept track of who had been on the national teams during the seven years he had coxed. He knew their names and was perpetually speculating about the selection, allowing that he personally did not expect to make the team that year. Coxswains, he said, were chosen finally on seniority, so he would have to get to know the people on the team for a year or two before earning a boat; but Andy was not looking ahead that far. [He was determined to earn a place on the team that year.] I too had told my friends that I was going for the experience, to see what the process was like in the hope of making an Olympic boat the following summer. I did not tell them that I believed that to be in Moscow in 1980, I would have to be in Bled in 1979.

Andy and I crossed the Connecticut River from Vermont into New Hampshire and started looking for the boathouse. As we crossed the bridge we spied the Harvard van pulling their shell trailer onto a dirt road. We gave chase and arrived at the boathouse moments later.

The Dartmouth crew was ill equipped compared to Harvard and Yale. They had what looked like an elongated three-door garage to house their shells and a single dock to launch them; but the Dartmouth equipment was not what caught my eye. Next to the boathouse was the Harvard trailer, loaded with sleek gleaming fours. Seat racing! I could already imagine Harry's voice from the launch. After a couple of short races in the four-oared shells, there would come the inevitable command, "Coxswains, pull the boats together!" As the boats paired off, drifting together, whispered speculation would begin to predict which pair of oarsmen would switch. As the boats came together, the two and four men of one boat would grab the blades of the two and four oars of the other boats pulling the boats together with each oarsman adjacent to his counterpart. Until the boats were meshed, nothing would be said from the coaches' launch; then, for another twenty seconds or perhaps even a minute, the coaches would confer. There would always be the pause before the announcement.

"Kiesling switch with Gardiner!" I already imagined the switch, me and the stroke of the Harvard eight.

As I untied my stretchers I would begin hyperventilating, gulping down air to store as much oxygen as

167

possible before the next piece. I would ache from previous races, but hearing my name would bring a fresh rush to my temples. Against the pounding I would glance into the boat beside me to measure my opponent. If he looked in worse shape, I would hurry so as not to allow him any extra time to rest, but if he looked less tired than me, I would take my time, fight down the panic. In silent unison we would switch boats, exchanging places and readjusting our new footstretchers while still following the "If he looks more tired then speed up" rule. Meanwhile, the others would have pushed the boats apart. Without a word from the coaches' launch, the boats would line up for the next race.

During the few strokes before the piece began, each boat would try to stay slightly more than even with the others without wasting too much of the energy necessary for the race. The boats would paddle faster and faster so that by the time Harry called "On this stroke!" we would be near full pressure. Everyone would then pull as if his future depended on that one race—because it often would. Theoretically, that race would be between Gordie and me because we were the two oarsmen to change places, but the process was more complex than that. Not only was it difficult to predict who would be switched next, but after a series of races with different combinations of oarsmen, one could be seat-raced without ever leaving the boat. Perhaps after one race we would go again without another switch. Perhaps not. All we would know was how the margin of victory changed from piece to piece. If I had switched from a winning boat and then won again, the seat race would be mine. If I switched from a losing boat and lost again, I would have lost. A few losses and one's name would not appear on the practice schedule. Few said good-bye.

Contemplating the shells on the trailer, I realized that it was not just fear that quickened my pulse. I felt a dreadful anticipation. At Yale I had only twice played this game of musical boats and it had never seemed to me that serious. We then called it the PROCESS (Preordained Rearrangement or Confused Existential Spatial Shifting) because it never seemed to turn out the way anyone expected or desired. I had always been processed successfully at Yale, but I had generally felt that even if I had lost, I would still have been in the first boat. A year under Tony's coaching would not be overturned in a day; but the camp was full of people who could beat me, people I would compete against not as a member of the Yale eight but as an individual. A loss for any reason could send me home.

Up a steep traverse of roots and evergreens from the boathouse we found the dormitory, an early-sixties, international-style bunker divided into cells for one and two freshmen. Inside, Pete Holland, the MIT coach, gave us keys to our room. He knew who we were but gave only a surly nod in response to our greeting. Most members of previous national teams were in their mid-twenties. The thought crossed my mind once again that we were just upstarts.

Outside on the lawn there were thirty or forty oarsmen clustered in small groups, the largest group being those of us from Yale. These were all college oarsmen like us. The big guns had not yet arrived. Looking around, I realized that for the moment we and the five Harvard oarsmen were the big guns. While untested, we were the next generation of team candidates.

At the meeting after dinner, there were more than one hundred oarsmen, considerably more than had been expected or could be accommodated. One hundred superior athletes, all over 6 feet tall and between 170 and 220 pounds. When Harry arrived it seemed that everyone else had rowed with him or was at least well acquainted. I was struck by the awe that he generated. At forty Harry was in superb shape. He was the U.S. single sculler in the 1960 Olympics and still had the look about him, a presence that withstood the worship of his followers. The Sprints and the Race had left the Yale eight on equal terms with Harry, but most everyone else in the room had either never beaten him or never lost with him. In his seventeen years at Harvard he had lost only a handful of races and his oarsmen had dominated the national team. Harry now spoke as if to talk at length to a group this large was a waste of his time. What I did not appreciate was that he would cut the group in half within thirty-six hours.

Harry told us that we were here to make "fast boats." We would stay so long as we appeared to make boats fast. Once it was clear that there were others who could make the boats faster, then we would leave. Those who were cut were free to ask why, but during the first few days there would be little time to answer.

Those first cuts, or "deselections," as one coach put it, would have nothing to do with seat racing. On the first day of selection, all one hundred of us were scheduled for an observational row in eights and an "ergometer piece." My row was scheduled at 8:30 the next morning and my erg piece at 3:00 in the afternoon. Without enough data yet to begin estimating my chances, I just went to sleep.

The next morning I was in an eight stroked by Joe, followed by Eric, me and Matthew. We did our best to look good, but by beating Harvard at the Sprints, I think we had guaranteed ourselves housing for at least the first few days. We rowed so that the four behind us could be evaluated; afterward we all went to breakfast to get acquainted. The next day those four all went home. I learned then to be cagey about whom I spent time with.

For those with good technique, the erg piece determined whether one could expect to be fed for long by Olympic development funds. Those who fared well were placed in the upper group for seat racing, those who did not do so well were in the lower group. Losing in the upper group dropped one to the lower group. From the lower group one went home.

The ergometer is a machine capable of measuring one's physical capabilities as an oarsman. The term "rowing machine" conjures up the junk advertised in mail-order athletic catalogs. An ergometer resembles that sort of rowing machine as an iron maiden resembles a corset. The modern ergometer was developed around 1970 by an ex-oarsman living near Stanford University who wanted a machine to simulate the resistance of pulling an oar through water that would measure the amount of energy he expended. After considerable time and expense he succeeded. After much less time, but great personal expense, he knew that he had created a monster. The creature was donated to Stanford, where it now sits, broken and despondent, but in the journey it managed to multiply. Second and third-generation machines now lurk in better boathouses all over the country.

In its resting position the ergometer is inscrutable. It stands on a roughly triangular base of 4-by-4 inch steel girders which supports the tracks of the sliding seat and an arm attached to a length of wooden oar. One rows on the machine as one rows a shell, but rather than having a uniform resistance against the sweep of the oar as in other rowing machines, the genius of the ergometer is that it harnesses the stroke to spin a massive steel flywheel. Momentum developed in the flywheel approximates the momentum of a shell. As if the flywheel were not difficult enough to keep spinning, there is a friction brake that rubs against the outside of the wheel. The pressure exerted by the brake is determined by the amount of weight placed in a small basket suspended from the brake arm, which in turn is a function of one's body weight. The heavier the oarsman, the more weight is placed in the basket. Sitting atop the cage housing the flywheel is a large darkroom-style timer, a tachometer and a counter. While the timer is running, the needle on the tachometer displays the speed of the flywheel and the counter records revolutions.

The ergometer simulates the physical demands of rowing, packaging the pains with none of the amenities that make it worthwhile—and the tachometer and counter keep you and everyone else around constantly aware of how hard you work and how fast you fade. Although it takes a long warm-up for an eight to swing, on an erg such subtleties don't matter. For me the sound alone raised my pulse to 120. Tying my feet into the stretchers increased it to 180. My maximum pulse was 200. I didn't need a warm-up. I needed a sedative.

At Yale we used ergometers to measure our progress during the fall and winter. When I was learning to row, these machines were the best indication that I would become a good oarsman. I came to enjoy their challenge. I was even eager to begin that piece at Dartmouth. It was to be a six-minute piece with six pounds suspended in the basket. For someone my weight, that combination was the equivalent of a 2,000-meter race.

The machines at Dartmouth had been moved for the testing to the medical center. An ominous move. That first piece, the coaches wanted our heart rates monitored; later, the tests became more sophisticated.

As I entered the hallway of the medical center I heard the sound. It began with a clank of the oar handle rising into the catch over the continuous whirring of the spinning flywheel, followed by a slight rattle of seat along the slide and the break-weight bouncing up and down as the wheel accelerated; then there was the *ping* of the release. *Clang...chtschtschtschts...chtsinnggg ...clang.* As I walked along the hallway the noise was getting louder. *Clank...chtschtscht....*I reached for the door, remembered the bathroom back down the hall and retreated.

When I was tied into the footstretchers, the coxswain gave me a little incentive. Biglow had pulled a score of 3785, the highest yet recorded on the port side. Anything over 3600 was good; in fact, there would only be three people over 3700 and seven or eight over 3600— until Otto pulled 4100, but he was not human.

Rowing on the machine, knowing that one's future as an oarsman hinged on that single effort, took the same mental preparation as did rowing a major race, but on the ergometer there was never the relief of realizing that the other boat was going to lose or the release of knowing that one's own boat was hopelessly behind. There was the clock, the counter and the tachometer needle. The clock moved through time as if the first seconds of the piece were no different from the last, the counter clicked, and the tach slipped backward down the scale. There was the pain, the tachometer and the occasional voice of a coxswain. Three thousand six hundred and eighty-five revolutions of the flywheel later, they all stopped.

The national team camp resembled Gales Ferry the way rowing on an ergometer resembles rowing a shell. At the camp all that mattered was fast boats: not tradition, not friendship, not personal growth, just fast boats. We sought diversion between practices, but only to kill time. There were interesting people, but the people and the entire experience were secondary to the goal. Until the boats were chosen, all considerations were personal.

If I bothered to think about it, I thought that we were treated like lab specimens. Often we treated each other like fellow specimens. When one of us proved to be less effective than another, he was discarded, forgotten. So long as we performed adequately, the coaches continued to post our names—the dining hall still maintained us.

As specimens we were monitored. I remember returning to that erg room a few days after my first piece. There were then about forty of us left, few enough that they could begin to scan our insides. My legs ached as I walked through the corridors filled with lab-coated medical technicians, and for a moment I was brought back to the familiar trudge into my freshman biology lab; this time, however, I was the white rat. The people doing the testing were acquaintances, people who had rowed on national teams before entering medicine, but that made the procedure seem no less threatening.

As in the previous piece, cardiac monitors were taped to my chest with the wires running out under my shirt. The oarsman ahead of me had to have a tuft of hair shaved from his chest to allow the tape to adhere. Glancing down at my own bare chest, I was about to make a comment about simian oarsmen when I noticed that I did have hair on my chest—one solitary three-quarter-inch strand in the middle of my sternum, which the doctor fastidiously shaved off. My hand was then placed in a bowl of warm water to dilate the capillaries. Simultaneously with pricking my finger, they stabbed the inside of my elbow. Measuring lactates in my blood, they told me, but I was so nervous that my blood refused to flow. Later they would try multiple lacerations of my earlobe.

Once on the ergometer, I was connected to a gas exchange monitor. They plugged my nose and inserted a snorkle into my mouth that was connected by flexible tubing to a couple of balloonlike plastic bags, which were in turn connected to a computer that spewed ticker tape. The mouthpiece was supported by a clear plastic frame connected to a headband. A valve in the snorkle allowed me to breathe outside air but exhale only into the machine, which would then measure the amount of oxygen I used and the amount of carbon dioxide I produced. Both these measurements gave an indication of how much work I could do.

The body, they told us, has both aerobic and anaerobic energy systems. The aerobic system burns the oxygen as it is absorbed through respiration, providing energy for steady work. The anaerobic system provides additional energy when the body is pushed beyond its aerobic capability; unfortunately, the anaerobic process is inefficient and produces lactic acid, the substance which causes sore muscles. Theoretically, people with high aerobic thresholds, those who can sustain high-intensity work for long periods of time before switching to the anaerobic system, are more efficient and are, therefore, more desirable oarsmen than those with low thresholds. What surprised me though was the disparity between the threshold values of different oarsmen. Some excellent oarsmen had relatively low thresholds. All that proves was that they had superior strength, better technique or a higher tolerance for pain. No matter how well one fared in the physiological testing, it would not make up for lost seat-races.

The month dragged by while my fate was being decided. During that time I had to keep reminding myself that I was there because I wanted to be. All I had to do was fail and I could go home. During those weeks our group from Yale was ripped apart. I wondered what had happened to the bonds that had formed during our season.

The first night of the camp Karl left. A poor erg and a frustrating row preceded the note on Matthew's door to say that it was over. He had not been cut, he just wanted to leave. Please say good-bye to everybody, I had to catch the bus, the note explained. I didn't see Karl again until September, when he dropped by the boathouse before leaving to spend the year at Trinity College, Dublin.

Two days later, Joe removed himself from the camp. His girl friend was taking courses at Dartmouth for the summer. She and the approach of medical school convinced him to drop out, although at the time Joe could quite possibly have made the team. I wonder if he would have. Joe wonders much more than I. He still plans to get back in shape to make one more try to find out where he stood.

Ted was the first of us to be cut. He was on the list from one hundred to fifty and from fifty to forty, but from forty to thirty-two his name was absent. I think he remembers the camp more fondly than the rest of us. He remained relaxed, met some of the people he had heard about, and found out how he stood. Ted has remained close to the crew, but he feels no pressure to try again.

At breakfast, a week into the camp, John told me that Eric was packing his bags. It didn't seem likely. He had not been doing as well as everyone expected, but even a mediocre performance for Eric was impressive. I left in search of him, finding him finally on the telephone asking about the bus schedule. Charlie Altecruse and I tried to convince him to stay. Altecruse, the Harvard four man to whom I had given my shirt in New London, was now helping me convince Eric that he ought not to leave.

Harry convinced Eric to stay, but three days later, he and Matthew were cut. Eric, who was later found to have the strongest legs on the entire Olympic rowing squad (stronger in test than even Eric Heiden's), and who went on to row the highest ergometer piece in the nation, convinced himself that he was not going to make it. Matthew rowed admirably for his two years of experience, but did not have the strength. He was told to lift weights for a few months and try again for 1980.

The survivors divorced themselves from the surroundings. We sank into ourselves, always awaiting that next practice, that next seat-race, that next list of those still in contention. Enthusiasm, excitement and psyche were dangerous. For every pinnacle there would be the trough. I learned to steel myself for practice without upsetting the rhythm of the day, avoiding confidence as well as fear. One came in contact mostly with those on the same level of the rowing hierarchy, and there

177

friendships were strained if not cut short. I avoided entanglements. For a long time neither Eric nor I had spoken to John because he had earned a seat early. Then Eric and I had stopped talking as my chances improved. Those days I spent my time with the pinball machine.

After the cut from thirty-two to twenty-four, I drove Eric to the bus station, but could think of nothing to say. The Yale eight seemed so very far away. He and I had about equal experience and capability so in one sense his departure made it easier for me to think of leaving, but I knew Biglow was going to make the team. I thought that I would look stupid writing a book about training for the Olympic team if my roommate was the only person from Yale selected.

The next morning the remaining twenty-four of us milled about in the doorway of the boathouse, fidgeting in the cool morning breeze, yet trying not to seem nervous. News had circulated that the top sixteen would be designated that morning. The eight, four-with-coxswain and spares would be chosen from the top sixteen oarsmen. The four-without-coxswain would be selected from the remaining eight oarsmen, but the four-without also had to win a trials race to go to Yugoslavia. Everyone was subdued yet joking to conceal the tension. I knew that I had been in the top sixteen until the previous afternoon, when I had either tied or lost to Steve Christiansen from Penn.

Without fanfare, Harry came down and called the names of those in the top group, eight starboard and eight port. With each name he called on the port side I winced, realizing that I was not going to make it. "Ibetsen, Otto, Espeseth, Purdy, Altecruse, Biglow." Two more spaces. "Clifford and Christiansen." Damn

Biglow, I thought to myself, as I walked off to take my place in the group from which the four-without would be chosen.

So much time and so much pain and still the odds were 50 percent, about the same as they had seemed from the beginning. I couldn't afford to feel sorry for myself, but the entire camp drifted into unpleasant unreality. The extended uncertainty seemed intolerable, but I knew then that I had no choice but to survive. My competition for the two seat of the four-without was Gordie Gardiner, the stroke from Harvard.

For the next two days the eight of us prepared for the final seat-racing between the two straight fours (a straight boat is one without a coxswain), but the boats refused to go straight. The rudder was connected by rope to one shoe on the bowman's footstretchers. The bowman steered by moving his foot from side to side, a process called toeing, but it took some time for the bowmen to develop their toes. In the meantime we toured the river randomly. Eventually, though, the boats settled themselves and we were ready. Gordie and I both knew that our time had come. After that practice one of us would pack his bags.

On the dock I discovered Marcella was gone. Marcella, an old Croker with a narrow worn grip, was my oar, the one I had grown fond of during the week. I had picked the blade randomly from the Harvard set and had then become accustomed to its peculiar feel. Using any of the other oars, I had tended to "wash out," but Marcella was pitched differently and seemed to compensate for whatever it was I had been doing wrong. I searched frantically in and around the boathouse and the trailers, but eventually had to grab a substitute and run to the dock.

In the warm-up I could barely keep the oar buried through the stroke. Even after I had wrapped several layers of black electrical tape around the upright of the oarlock, the pitch was still wrong, but I knew that to complain would only decrease the level of confidence in the boat. Without knowing the extent of my handicap, we rowed to the line for the first race, a four-minute piece at 34 strokes per minute.

The boats paddled together, picking up speed, and then we were off. Normally each boat would take three strokes to build the rating, ten strokes at a higher cadence to set the tone, and then the rating would settle to a more manageable rate. Three, ten and settle to 34 strokes per minute, we were told by the coach. If either boat did not settle after ten strokes or settled above 34 strokes per minute the coach would make us begin again. To be fair, the stroke ratings had to be the same in the two boats; but no one in my boat thought twice before deciding that we would count five strokes instead of three before officially calling the ten. Not settling until after a total of fifteen strokes rather than thirteen might gain us an extra few feet. Whether it helped or not, when we settled we were a seat ahead. By the end of the piece we led by almost two lengths.

"Pull the boats together!"

And so the boats pulled together and Gardiner and I each got ready to send the other home, but when the boats were together I noticed that he was rowing with Marcella. Great! I thought to myself, now it would be mine for the next piece. But Gardiner opened his oarlock and demanded that we switch oars as well as boats. I learned later that he too had been using Marcella during the week, but I had never heard of anyone switching oars in a seat race. There would be no way to know if the pitch of the oarlock was compatible, but it seemed no time to argue.* Angrily I removed my oar and stepped across, hoping that the tape I had left on the oarlock would leave the boat unrowable. Marcella obviously didn't help him because he lost the next two pieces by more than a length.

News that the Yalie had beaten Harvard spread rapidly through the camp, and for the moment I felt as if I had single-handedly avenged the Harvard race. Grace had allowed me a second chance and I had succeeded. To earn that victory, however, I rose above myself to perform at a level higher than I could sustain, knowing all the while that the peak would have to be paid for. I collapsed at the end of the practice, assuming that at least temporarily the pressure would be off.

*Much later I learned that Harvard oarsmen were accustomed to switching oars during seat races. At Harvard, oarsmen kept the same oar all year rather than changing oars when they change seats.

A Different Symphony

Grace, in another form, also gave Gordie a second chance. Immediately after the practice, he argued that the results of the seat racing were not reliable because the boats had been so erratic in the previous practices. In any case, he argued, we had been at the camp so long that the results of any one practice should not be decisive. Before the next practice, Finley Meislen, the coach of the straight four, told me that there was some possibility that I would be switched again. I knew then that when the boats were pulled together, Gordie and I would be the only changes.

Why would they let him try again unless they wanted him to win? I thought to myself as I went down to practice. Finley told me that because I had won the first time, I would be given the seat unless there were a dramatic reversal from the previous practice, but I was nervous and frightened. It occurred to me that the coaches might want to keep Gordie rowing with us until the remainder of the four was selected, but that seemed unlikely. After all, Gordie was from Harvard. I felt as if once more I had to face Randy on the fifty-yard line.

When we went down to row, the business with the oars continued. I never saw Marcella until the boats were pulled together and Gordie and I were told to switch. Once again he refused to give it up. My four had won the first race, but I was not thinking clearly and had wasted most of my reserve energy trying to increase the margin in the last few strokes. As we switched seats, I was scared. I wanted to reach out and grab Marcella, just to deprive him of it.

Gordie, more than anyone other than Harry Parker, had engineered our loss at the Ferry; and now a strange, unreasoning dread told me once again that something was badly wrong—although rationally I believed I was where I wanted to be. Because my boat had won the first race, I needed only to tie the second to win.

A five-minute seat race is a long way, almost a mile, and only one minute short of the standard 2,000 meters. Five minutes seemed infinitely more painful than the four-minute pieces of the day before, and five strokes into the piece I realized that I did not have the concentration. Powered by hatred and fear, I could not relax. Just like the Harvard race, I thought in a wave of nausea, but when I tried to relax, the boat became sluggish. Gordie's boat began inching away.

The other four appeared to be moving away faster than it actually was because the boats were converging slightly. Because our boat tended to pull a bit to the starboard side and the other boat pulled a little to port, soon the blades from the two shells were only inches apart, and we were two seats down and then three. Coming into the last minute, though, we pulled back and finished even. Once again victory was mine, but the margin was smaller. I prayed that the coach would switch another pair of oarsmen to indicate that my victory had been telling, but instead he made us line up for the next piece. I had won three times, but one loss would throw the entire series into question.

Two minutes into the next piece, the boats were even but my body was giving way. A muscle in my chest which I had pulled early in the season began to knot and then my legs started to cramp. The shirt on the man in front of me melted in a swirl of red and blue revolving in the flow of oars. My head, which was usually erect and focused on the shoulders of the man in front, lolled from side to side. With two minutes left in the piece, it occurred to me with an impersonal clarity that I did not have seventy strokes left in me—maybe ten and maybe twenty, but not a full two minutes worth. Perhaps that was how Pete felt when he refused the last race at Yale. I was going to lose that piece and any subsequent piece I would row.

The four was again veering to starboard only a few feet from the blade tips of the other boat when mine began to fall back. I have only ten more strokes, I thought in despair. Ten more strokes...Instantly, I changed my technique. As we became more tired, we tended to decrease the length of our strokes, but now I reached out beyond the normal limit and then gave what I thought was a tremendous surge at the end of the stroke. I counted these strange new strokes as once again the shells faded into the whirl of color. One, two, three. The boat staggered. At any moment it would die. Four, five. I glanced over to starboard but could not focus. I could hear the coach yelling directions frantically from the launch. Our bowman awoke to the danger, and called for the port side to ease, but he too must have seen the escape because he did not turn the rudder. Nine, and then on the tenth stroke, the blades of the two boats tangled in a splintering crash—dead even with one minute left in the race. That night Gordie packed his bags.

A week later, Paul Prioleau, Dave Kehoe, John (Twig) Terwilliger, our coach Finley Meislen and I put our four on the trailer and drove to the trials at Princeton to race the University of Pennsylvania and Vesper Boat Club for the right to go to the World Championships. In the other straight fours were members of previous national teams who, having been cut from the camp, returned to their clubs to train for the trials. They began practicing two weeks before our four had even been selected, but having survived the camp, we knew that we should win. Tired of uncertainty and annoyed that we had to race against oarsmen whom we had beaten individually at the camp, we stenciled on the backs of our racing shirts our new logo—a picture of two vultures and the words PATIENCE MY ASS, WE'RE GONNA KILL SOMETHING! Five hundred meters into the race we led by a seat. At a thousand meters, when we already led by a length of open water, we raised the rating and then raised it again with five hundred meters to go. We won by six boat lengths, a "time zone," and paddled back to the deck to be outfitted with the blue shirts with red-and-white sashes of the United States National Rowing Team.

John Terwilliger, the three man of the straight four, came from nowhere and made the team. A large, lean cowboy from Wyoming, Twig decided that he wasn't working hard enough at the nearly nonexistent rowing program at Seattle Pacific University, so he packed himself into his car, turned on the tape deck, and headed east. He arrived in Boston in the middle of May because he had heard that Harry planned to coach a group in preparation for the national camp. Everyone else in the group had heard of everyone else at least by reputation, but no one had yet heard of the Twig.

Harry took him out for a few practices in Cambridge and then told him to try again the next year, but because Twig had driven three thousand miles, Harry led him down to the Harvard rowing tanks to show him some technical points to work on back in Seattle. Twig took a seat in the vacant tank room and started to row. After twenty minutes Harry left to coach the next practice. Several hours later, when Harry was in his office finishing up, an oarsman came to the door. Someone, he told Harry, was rowing in the tanks and wanted to know if he could stop. No one is sure how long Twig rowed that day, but if he had been on a straight course, he might have made it back to Wyoming. Harry told him to show up for practice the next morning.

Biglow, who had initially hated me for being inexperienced, considered Twig's success outside the realm of decency. Initially, there was little contact between the two because John stayed with the eight, but only a few days after we arrived in Yugoslavia, John fell ill with a sudden and malingering virus. He turned pale, lost weight, and eventually had to be replaced by one of the spare oarsmen. For fear of infecting anyone else, he roomed alone and often dined at his own table. I don't know if his sudden vulnerability made him recede into himself or whether he felt that the team abandoned him as soon as he could no longer row; whatever the reason, the illness took the heart out of him. After a couple of attempts to get back in the boat, he resigned himself to life on the bank. That was when he, Dave Kehoe, Twig and I began our nightly hearts game.

John and I had often played hearts, a card game somewhat like bridge, before races at Yale, and we convinced Twig and Dave to join us. The object of the game was not to take any hearts unless one managed to take all the hearts and the queen of spades. All was well so long as Twig sat quietly losing, but once he shot the moon and beat us all. It was after the first hand on our second night of play when I asked Dave how many hearts he had.

"None."

"John, how many do you have?"

"None."

"Well, I don't have any either," I said in disbelief, looking over at Twig, who was counting his cards.

"I have thirteen hearts and I picked up the queen," he said ruefully. "How many points is that?"

"Twig, that means you won."

John stalked off in a rage. Thrashing Twig at cards had been one way for John to emphasize subtly that Twig was an outsider and to ease his own mounting frustration at not being able to row. To be beaten by me at cards was bad, but to be beaten by Twig was too much. For the remainder of the trip John went out of his way to prod Twig's already short temper, until the night after the finals Twig finally lost control and punched him in the nose.

Before he went to the camp, John thought that the national team would be the ultimate team, that we would have so much in common that the individuals would be a more cohesive group than even the Yale crew had been. The national team boats were rowed so well that we could use the pronouns "I" and "we" interchangeably when describing a set of strokes. When we rowed, I wasn't conscious of others; instead, I was conscious of the amplification of my own strength by the others, but John thought that we would have that same unity outside the shells. At the camp and especially after he got sick, John learned that the intimacy he expected was more commonly a single-minded dedication to looking after ourselves. Because Twig was different from the rest of us, his presence exemplified the failure of John's expectations. John hated Twig because he didn't seem to know how to look out for himself; however, when I was arrested by the militia while climbing the flagpole, Twig stayed close to make sure nothing happened to me.

As I followed Twig and the others up the stairs to our rooms one night after another hearts game, I thought of how different we were from the Yale crew. We were better oarsmen with higher expectations, but we hadn't grown up together. We came together fully formed and served one another as the next step toward a personal excellence. Being in the company of the best would bring out the best in us individually, but we were all too conscious of ourselves to be melded into a whole greater than the sum of its parts. We raced together on that clear mountain lake in Bled with the castle on the cliff and the island with the little Romanesque chapel, but we didn't know what or whom we were racing for. My goal had been to make the team, and I had never thought beyond that. Against Gordie I had carried the banner of Yale, but afterward I had earned a place on this new team, a team which, rather than providing a direction, provided only a vehicle for our own individual directions.

Halfway through our first heat in the World Championships we were in second place and moving on the leading four, but when the time came to sprint, we lost heart and dropped back to third. On the following day, a crab in the start of the repechage heat, our second chance to qualify for the semifinals, put us a length behind the other five boats, and it was only the shame of not qualifying that brought us together to win. When on the third day of racing we paddled out to the semi-finals, no one expected our boatload of rookies to earn a place in the finals. Tension was high in the boat; in fact, I think we hated each other, but I knew that when we channeled that hatred into rowing the boat, we lifted it out of the water and flew. During one ten-stroke piece, Twig made us so angry that we spelled out the only ten-letter obscenity, calling one letter at each stroke. Afterward, I thought that if we could harness that energy for 2,000 meters, we could beat the East Germans. As it turned out, however, we failed to qualify for the finals, and finished the next day second in the Petit Finals, or eighth in the world. I left Yugoslavia wanting to get back to my friends at Yale, but mostly eager to start training for the 1980 Olympics.

Epilogue

"Was it really necessary for you to leave Yale to make the Olympic team?" It was the second time he had asked the question, but I hadn't been paying attention.

I sank back into the armchair, letting my eyes play back and forth between Biglow and the reporter. It all seemed so blessedly far away. There were still unanswered questions, but a reporter, even this Old Blue, was not the person to ask them. They were Biglow's and mine and even we hadn't settled our accounts, but we might ignore them if they weren't forced upon us. I tried once more to think back. Grandma Biglow then entered with a tray of cookies, but as I took a couple I began to wonder whether she knew of the rift between me and her grandson. Had I abandoned him?

I hadn't seen John since July, 1980, when the U.S. Olympic Rowing Team split up after a month of racing in Europe, which because of the boycott had been two weeks before the opening ceremonies of the Moscow Olympics. Now the leaves were golden through the window. When we shook hands John still had the same familiar grip, but smooth palm met smooth palm. We had graduated from Yale but neither of us had jobs or even plans for finding them, and the thought of going back to school was very distant indeed. Chance found us together at Grandma Biglow's for our first attempt to sort out the last few months. Somewhere along the way we had picked up this old alumnus who thought he might be able to write a story about the two Yale Olympians in the class of 1980.

"To put the question another way, what finally made you decide to go to the camp for the Olympic eight rather than row in the straight four trials in the Yale boat?" I grabbed another cookie and sat back to think.

John and I returned to Yale from Yugoslavia in September of 1979. There had been only three undergraduates on the 1979 national team, so John and I were undisputably the big names of college rowing. Eric and Matthew had both been in the top thirty-two oarsmen in the country, and Andy Messer had rowed on the Canadian national team. Even when Andy left Yale to train with the Canadian Olympic squad, Yale still had four oarsmen training for the U.S. Olympic team, and was again destined to clobber everyone. The problem was both to clobber everyone and still make the Olympic team.

There were two possible ways to make the Olympic rowing team: by succeeding in the selection camp for the eight and four-with-coxswain or by winning the trials for the straight four. Since there were the four of us at Yale, all of whom were in the top thirty-two in the country, and we had been rowing together for years, rowing in the trials seemed the most elegant solution. In October, 1979, we got an indication of how good a four we had when we won the Head of the Charles, the largest regatta of the fall, by almost thirty seconds. Not only could we win the trials, I thought, but we could win a medal in Moscow.

November marked the beginning of selection for the Olympic camp. One hundred oarsmen from the East Coast converged at Princeton, and another fifty met at Berkeley, California, for a weekend of ergometer pieces and seat racing so that Harry Parker could select fifty oarsmen for the funded Olympic training squad. The squad would be brought together regularly for physiological testing and additional seat-racing until May, 1980, when the eight and coxed four would be selected from the final camp. Eric, Matthew, John and I missed the Harvard-Yale football game so that we could row ergometer pieces in the Princeton boathouse, yet the trip might have been completely for the best (Yale lost the football game) had Matthew not failed to qualify for the training squad. When we returned to Yale, Eric and I had dreams of making the eight, while John, who had developed a serious pain in his lower back, was remembering how miserable he had been in the eight in Yugoslavia.

The boycott, which was announced tentatively in January, 1980, had little effect on the early selection process. In order to protest the boycott, one had to be confident that he would still be on the team in May, and few were that confident. The majority of us did our best to ignore the issue, realizing that the sense of futility engendered by the boycott would hurt our chances of making the team. The first tangible effect of the boycott was to accelerate the selection schedule so the team could race in Lucerne in June rather than Moscow in July. Changing the schedule made it impossible to compete with Yale in the trials and, if we lost, still go to the camp; instead, we had to choose.

Tony feared our indecision could divide the Yale crew. He preferred that we go to the trials because we would then not travel to Cambridge every other weekend to row for Harry Parker, but more important than what we decided was that we make a decision quickly. Unfortunately, that decision depended on how well we were doing at any given time.

Matthew's only chance of being on the Olympic team had been to row in the trials, and for that reason he was not part of the decision. For Eric the decision was initially difficult, but it was finally made for him. During the winter he was at the very top of the Olympic squad and was in favor of the camp. Having been cut from the camp at Dartmouth, Eric wanted to prove that he could make the Olympic team on his own; although out of loyalty he said that he would join us in the trials if we needed him. He helped convince John and me to continue with the camp, but then, inexplicably, Eric began losing seat races. Even though he had been the strongest man during the physiological testing, by April Eric learned that he would not be one of the twenty oarsmen invited to the final selection camp.

Matthew and Eric eventually had no choice but to row in the trials, and then John, who was virtually guaranteed a seat in one of the camp boats, decided that he wanted to row the straight four. He had such a miserable time in Yugoslavia that he wanted to make the team only if he were rowing with friends. He counted on me to row with them, but I was still undecided. I had been a proponent of going to the trials during the winter, but after I won a few more seat races in Cambridge, I knew my chances were better with the camp. Eventually, I decided the camp was more important, and Dave Potter replaced me in the four.

Pleadingly, I looked at John, who smiled. "When I asked my father whether he thought I should row in the trials or go to the camp, he advised that it is often better to lose in good company," I said, with some hesitation. My gaze had landed inadvertently on the banner of the '07 Yale football team. "He was never really an athlete, though."

I didn't know if that would be sufficient explanation for the reporter, but John knew what I meant and we smiled sadly at each other. The look was not lost upon the reporter, who tried to appear sympathetic. He thought we were thinking about the trials race.

Graduation day, a few days after I had earned my seat on the Olympic team, I picked up my diploma while Eric, John, Matthew and Dave rowed the race that determined that they would not be on the Olympic team. The trials had not been close. As in 1979, when my four had gone to the trials, the last four oarsmen from the Olympic camp put together a straight four, and they won by six seconds. John later joined the team unofficially as a replacement for Otto, who had hurt his back.

"I knew the Yale four was going to lose the trials," I answered finally.

John looked up questioningly. I had never told him that. Even if I instead of Dave Potter had rowed in the Yale four, it would have lost. I probably should have told John that when I made my decision to leave the four, but then I did not know why it was that the four would lose. I just knew. I also didn't want John to come with me to the camp. He would have beaten me, and I came near enough to being cut.

"John, remember how I was when I rowed in the trials race before we went to Yugoslavia?"

John nodded, so I turned to the reporter to explain.

"I had been seat-racing at the camp for weeks before I earned the right to row in the trials. The four of us were not that good, but we won easily because we had been through so much to get there. We had no choice but win. You remember our racing shirts for that race, don't you, John?"

John smiled ruefully. "The shirts were yellow tank tops with 'USA JUNIOR VARSITY' across the front, and a patch on the back with two vultures and our slogan, 'PATIENCE MY ASS, WE'RE GONNA KILL SOMETHING!'"

"The Yale boat had the talent to beat the four from the camp, but you could come home to Yale if you lost. It was still a college boat even though the oarsmen were of national team caliber."

"So what made you so different?" the reporter interjected, with a look that I thought was accusing, but that could have been my imagination.

"My ability to row was no different," I answered, "but my approach was different. When the four from the camp went to the trials, they believed that they had each earned the right to be on the team, and if that right were taken away, they would have spent the year and accomplished nothing. Mother Yale would welcome her four sons home no matter what happened at the trials, but the camp four had nothing to return to—not even each other. That awareness was the six seconds that separated those two boats."

"I can understand how they felt that way after training

196

with Harry all that time in Boston, but what about you? You didn't have to give up that much."

"I may have given up a lot more than I bargained for," I answered, realizing at the same time that it was true. "I was physically and emotionally exhausted after we lost the Sprints to Harvard. It was never really a race after the crab during the start of the finals, yet the next day I had to be at Harvard for the final Olympic selection camp. There, I lost seat races that I should have won, but I could hardly bear to row. By going to the camp, I believed I had abandoned my friends and my school. For four years my identity had been defined by the Yale crew, but when I left, I did not believe I would ever be accepted back. I had to admit that the only possible reason I was rowing was for myself, and for quite some time I didn't feel that I was worth working for. If I could have come back to Yale without making the Olympic team, I probably would have." As I uttered the last sentence, I knew that I was lying.

I had seen the trials as a morally acceptable escape, a way of transferring some responsibility for my own fate to others, but there had never really been a choice. The escape was a trap. Joe fell into it at the 1979 national camp when he thought that being with his girl friend was more important than discovering whether he had the stuff to make the team, and now he is rowing his way through medical school in the hope fate will give him another chance. John also tried the escape with the four, but he did so because he misjudged the importance of the team. He told me before the trials that if the four lost, he would consider himself unworthy of the team. The only aspect of his character that made him "unworthy" was the thought that his own worthiness could be put into even his best friends' hands. He realized that after he lost the trials. I made the team because ultimately I had no doubts about who I was rowing for. If I had, I would not be an Olympian.

"But having made the Olympic team, how can you say that you gave up more than you bargained for?"

I looked over at John, wondering how he would answer that question, but his eyes were far away. I followed his gaze upward to the picture of his grandfather's eight on the Thames.

In 1906 the Race had been upstream just as it had my junior year; in 1980, however, the Race was switched so that we finished rather than began at the Bridge. Other than the direction, the Race was as it had always been, but for Biglow and me it was also our last duty before leaving with the Olympic team. The camp had left me feeling distant from my crew and the camaraderie of the Ferry, but I had thought the distance might be an advantage. I could approach the Ferry as just another camp and the Race as just another seat race; in fact, I chose to wear the shorts given to me by the Olympic team rather than Yale's. Harvard's latest stroke would fall as Gordie Gardiner had fallen from the camp a year before.

A mile into the race we had been a length up and were rowing two strokes lower than Harvard. Awesome! At a mile and a half gone we were still rowing easily when we fluttered the rating up two beats for ten high strokes to break away. The move worked splendidly and broke open water between us and Harvard. Open water, I knew, would be the crucial difference over the year before.

At two miles gone we were two lengths up, two strokes lower and moving away. Harvard looked terrible. They thrashed about so badly that even Altecruse was admitting defeat. Then they started moving back, although at three miles gone we still led by almost two lengths.

"John, do you know what happened?"

"Not really," he said vacantly. I did not know either, and during our month together in Europe we avoided the subject.

Somehow Harvard either sped up in the last three-quarters of a mile or we slowed down. They went through us pretty quickly and it seemed that we could do nothing to stop them, as if we had no strength left. There were two Olympians in our boat and two more who had just missed the team, but still we were beaten. If the whole boat had been Olympians, then skill and our own total concern with ourselves would have kept the boat together in the last mile. If we had no Olympians in that boat, our eight could have risen beyond its parts to hang together in the last mile, just as the junior varsity had done. But we were a mixed boat and never really a crew. Nine individuals panicked. When Tony had warned me that it would be difficult to row for both Yale and the national team, I had thought he had been worried about the logistical problems of competing with two different teams. Unfortunately, the real problems did not become overwhelming until the final test.

"Well, I have got to go now," said the alumnus, as he picked himself up from the chair. "Before I leave, though, could I have some quote from you guys about what it is like to be on the Olympic team?"

I cringed. This is the point where all athletes ultimately sound like idiots. At least we were not out of breath with a microphone shoved under our noses, but my mind was blank. Biglow was often good at rattling off innocuous clichés to satisfy the reporters, but I hoped we could do better. When he now spoke I was dismayed, but the more I thought about it, the more appropriate it seemed. Perhaps it struck me only because he used the same glowing cliché my junior high school track coach had used when he described what he thought it meant to be an Olympic athlete. I then had no conception of what my coach really meant, nor, I think, did he. I don't know if I just imagined the trace of irony when Biglow pontificated, "The Olympian stands alone." Before we parted, Biglow and I agreed to race a double scull in the Head of the Charles.